Unhackable will teach you why ~~off-course for years, decades, o~~ protect yourself and then beco.

—**Dr. Benjamin Hardy**, author of
Willpower Doesn't Work and *Personality Isn't Permanent*

The most successful athletes and high performers are Unhackable. Becoming Unhackable in work and life requires us to embrace Chosen Suffering. Kary's new book is a roadmap for how to get there.

—**Tom Ryan**, NCAA Wrestling Head Coach for The Ohio State University National Championship Team and author of *Chosen Suffering*

Kary has given us a perfect mix of art, science, and practical application that we can use in our companies to truly reach our most desired state, happiness! This is a proven formula for embracing a more exciting and effortless life.

—**Jill Young**, CEO of TractionFirst, Certified EOS Implementer®, and author of *The Advantage Series*

I help the highest performers achieve a Category of One status in the marketplace. No one gets to that place in life or business without learning how to become Unhackable.

—**Mike Koenigs**, serial entrepreneur, author, speaker

Kary has written an incredible resource that can be applied to almost any area of our lives. We all get hacked, but what's more important is our response—know your culprit and set your strategy. Buy this book as a resource for the critical comeback moments in your life!

—**Dean Fulks**, lead pastor Lifepoint Church, author of *Your Next 30 Days*

If anyone can show you how to protect your mind from Big Tech, it's Kary Oberbrunner. Get this book and read it today.

—**Jim Edwards**, bestselling author of *Copywriting Secrets* and co-founder of Funnel Scripts

If ever there was a book for our times, this is it! Get *Unhackable*, then feel and live the difference it makes in a heartbeat.

—**Paul Dunn**, 4-time TEDx speaker, serial entrepreneur and chairman of B1G1, creating over 200M giving impacts worldwide

Several years ago, Kary and I took a group of people through our Escaping Shawshank experience. We awakened those participants to their dreams and possibilities in an intense exercise now captured with clarity in *Unhackable*. The message remains: "Get busy living or get busy dying." (Andy Dufresne) Be prepared to write your Boon Check and become the person you were born to be.

—**Dan Miller,** New York Times bestselling author, *48 Days to the Work You Love*

Unhackable is a wake-up call for anyone online. Kary shows us how to navigate the noise, create a life of meaning, and achieve our dreams.

—**Rachel Pedersen,** Social Media and Digital Marketing Strategist

I used to wonder, *How does Kary accomplish all that he does but still have time for the things that are most important to him like his family, his friends, and his faith?* Well, I don't have to wonder any longer because, in *Unhackable*, I've got a front-row seat to Kary's high-performance secrets (and so do you!). Kick distraction to the curb once and for all. Read *Unhackable* now!

—**Jeff Brown**, podcaster and author of the forthcoming book *Read to Lead*

A must-read! *Unhackable* provides the motivation and method for you to awaken your dormant dreams and systematically make them a reality. Kary Oberbrunner generously provides his experience and roadmap to help you achieve your goals.

—**Skip Prichard**, CEO, Speaker, Wall Street Journal bestselling author of *The Book of Mistakes: 9 Secrets to Creating a Successful Future*

Dreams were never meant to stay mentally in our heads. Dreams were entrusted to us, so we create them physically with our hands. Unhackable gives us a practical process for achieving our dream without getting derailed by distractions.

—**Mark Batterson**, New York Times bestselling author of *The Circle Maker*, Lead Pastor of National Community Church

In present and future times, those who disrupt the world for good will be labeled as those who are unhackable. Every aspiring world changer should make *Unhackable* mandatory reading.

—**Paul C. Brunson**, Business Columnist for *USA Today*, Television Host, International Entrepreneur, personally endorsed by Oprah

It's a rare thing to read a new manuscript and know that you are actually experiencing a classic work of art. The truths in *Unhackable* are timeless and transformative!

—**Joshua Finley**, pastor and author of *Overcome*

We are all on a search for purpose and meaning in life, however along the way we get hacked and our dreams derailed. In *Unhackable*, Kary offers up a research driven formula to rediscover what you were born for and reignite your dreams into reality.

—**Casey B. Weade**, CEO and author of *Job Optional**

We are constantly being hacked with distractions, negativity, and shiny objects that can derail us from executing on our dreams for extended periods of time. That is until now! Kary has created a blueprint for anyone to build their *Unhackable* life and put their dreams into action."

—**Chris White**, author, host of *Tractionville* Podcast, and Certified EOS Implementer®

If you're disengaged and dissatisfied with your life, you've probably been hacked (and you're not alone). *Unhackable* is THE transformational blueprint for reclaiming your time, your energy, and your life.

—**Jon Giganti**, podcaster

True strength, happiness, and success comes when we're able to connect with our highest and best self. For any person on that journey, it takes a lot of focus and energy to work through past traumas, societal programming, and daily distractions. Kary lays out a great roadmap on how to reconnect with our purest core beliefs to create a strong, Unhackackable foundation for growth.

—**Brett Kaufman**, Founder & CEO of Kaufman Development and Host of the *Gravity* podcast

UNHACKABLE

Also by Kary Oberbrunner

Elixir Project
Day Job to Dream Job
The Deeper Path
Your Secret Name
The Fine Line
Called
The Journey Towards Relevance

UNHACKABLE

CLOSE THE GAP BETWEEN
DREAMING AND DOING

The 30-Day Elixir for Creating Flawless Ideas,
Leveraging Superhuman Focus, and Achieving Optimal
Human Performance Through Flow

KARY OBERBRUNNER

ethos
collective

Published by Ethos Collective
P.O. Box 43, Powell, OH 43065
ethoscollective.vip

Library of Congress Cataloging: 2020919627

Paperback: 978-1-63680-000-4
Hardback: 978-1-63680-001-1
Ebook: 978-1-63680-002-8

Available in hardcover, softcover, e-book, and audiobook.

To all those who got hacked.
They died with their song still inside them.
They don't have another chance.
You do.

And to the Igniting Souls Leadership Team:
Brenda Haire, Amanda Painter, Abigail Young, Debra
Hayes, Brenda Dunagan, and Jill Young.
You are strong where I am weak.

CONTENTS

Foreword by Dan Sullivan xvii

A Note to You—the Reader xxi

The Unhackability Assessment xxv

Introduction xxvii

PART 1
UNVEILING

Day 1—Story: Write Your Story 3

Day 2—Desire: Pick Your Boon 18

Day 3—Culprit: Identify Your Culprit 25

Day 4—Conspiracy: Confront Your Conspiracy 32

Day 5—Cost: Count Your Cost 37

PART 2
IDEA: FLAWLESS IDEA ANATOMY

Day 6—Promise: Claim your Promise 45

Day 7—Promotion: Inventory Your Promotion 52

Day 8—Progress: Track Your Progress 62

Day 9—Posture: Strengthen Your Posture 69

Day 10—Creation: Create Your Idea 75

Day 11—Time: Write Your Check. 82

Day 12—Space: See Your Space 91

PART 3
FOCUS: DELIBERATE MAGNETIC FOCUS

Day 13—Urgency: Establish Your Deadline 99

Day 14—Agency: Choose Your Inputs. 118

Day 15—Energy: Allocate Your Attention 124

Day 16—Alignment: Align Your Assets 131

Day 17—Attraction: Open Your Eyes 137

Day 18—Amplification: Amplify Your Impact 145

Day 19—Activation: Activate Your DIET 156

PART 4
FLOW: OPTIMAL HUMAN PERFORMANCE

Day 20—Characteristics: Optimize Your Performance . . . 167

Day 21—Self: Silence Your Critics. 180

Day 22—Cycle: Unpack Your Cycle 189

Day 23—Mastery: Embody Your Mastery 197

Day 24—Neurochemicals: Engage Your eurochemicals . . 203

Day 25—Triggers: Understand Your Triggers 208

Day 26—Assessment: Assess Your Growth 219

PART 5
BOON

Day 27—Clarify: Clarify Your Boon 227

Day 28—Craft: Craft Your Boon 235

Day 29—Communicate: Communicate Your Boon . . . 244

Day 30—Creation: Create Your Boon 248

APPENDICES

Notes 259

Acknowledgments 271

About the Author 273

About the Publisher 274

About Igniting Souls 276

Your Next Steps with *Unhackable* 278

FOREWORD

Two particular experiences from my youth have had a transformative impact on my life.

I grew up on a farm in northern Ohio in the early 1950s. From a young age, I developed a unique skill to *think about my thinking*, which I attribute to the opportunities I had as an often-solitary fifth child of seven children to spend time on my own.

When I was eleven years old, I went for a walk on a chilly February day. Cornstalks crackled underfoot as I walked the field alone with my thoughts. I gazed at the beautiful blue sky and heard the distant noise of a DC-6 plane. At the time, planes often flew overhead on routes from New York to Chicago and then back again.

On that particular day, I followed the plane's progress across the sky. All of a sudden, I was hit with a thought—*I wonder how far I can go.*

That thought has stuck with me ever since. I believe we're always in the process of answering the question, *How far can I go?* I know the day I finally have an answer is the day I stop growing.

Since this incident, I've never felt lonely or separated. It's as close to a religious experience as I've ever had.

The second transformational experience took place after high school when I participated in an Outward Bound expedition in Scotland. Our instructors accompanied us on grueling physical challenges that involved hiking through mountain ranges.

One day, after days of carrying heavy packs up and down hilly terrain, I let my pack slide off my back and sat down on the ground, unsure if I wanted to take another step.

One of the instructors spotted me and asked a perplexing question: "Is this where you stop?" I was unsure how to answer and said, "What do you mean?"

He replied, "Everybody stops somewhere. Is this where you stop?"

I thought for a moment and then wiped the beads of sweat from my forehead. I glanced at the hill in front of us.

"No," I said. "This is not where I stop."

I grabbed my pack and hoisted it up. I walked day after day, committed to not stopping again for longer than a brief rest.

At the end of our trip, that same instructor approached me and said, "If you had stopped on the hill that day, your life would have been difficult. You would have been tempted to quit anytime you faced a struggle in the future."

He was right.

Since that day, whenever I confront a difficult decision in life or business, I ask myself, *Is this where I stop?* I've always answered that question with a resounding *no*.

The truth is, I know I can go further.

These two significant life experiences have influenced my attitudes and shaped my perspective. For the past seventy-six years, my approach to life has been to use my past experiences as new lessons in the present—and to use today to create bigger future experiences.

You're about to read an insightful book from my friend Kary Oberbrunner. After collaborating with him over the past two years, I can say that he identifies with these two transformational experiences from my youth. He thinks about his thinking and asks himself both of these questions regularly:

How far can I go?
Is this where I stop?

The answer to these two questions has led Kary on a deep journey. Over the past six years, he has explored what it means to become Unhackable. In our age of increasing distractions, he has discovered a process to close the gap between dreaming and doing.

Too many people come up with a great idea but get sidelined and sabotaged. Kary will show you how to create flawless ideas, leverage superhuman focus, and achieve optimal performance through flow.

If you're committed to creating a bigger future, this book will stretch your thinking.

—Dan Sullivan,
Co-Founder of Strategic Coach®,
known as the world's foremost expert on entrepreneurship,
author of *Who Not How.*

A NOTE TO YOU—THE READER

This book should have been released four years ago—at least, that was the plan. Just one problem.

I got hacked.

I know, I know, I can hear you saying, "The author of *Unhackable* got hacked?" I think it's a little ironic too. But it's the truth. And if that discredits me in your eyes, well, then stop reading because this book isn't for you.

I'm aiming for the opposite effect—that you find hope in my confession. After all, if I understand the intricacies of getting hacked firsthand, then I'll approach this important topic with honesty and empathy, not judgment and condemnation.

So, in this book, if you'll allow me, I take on the posture of your coach, not your critic. I'm the truth-teller who's rooting for you more than you'll ever understand.

Why? You might wonder.

Simple—because the stakes are so high.

Here's a peek into that premise.

"What's the most damaging thing in the life of a child?"

I wasn't ready for the question my friend Chet asked me.

Although I had no clue, I was even less prepared for the answer he gave. According to famed Swiss psychologist Carl Jung, the answer is, "The unlived life of the parent."

That may be true, but it doesn't help us. Stating the problem without providing an answer is cruel at best. Last time I checked, no parent wakes up and says, "Today, my goal is to live the *unlived life.*"

Whether or not you have kids, the analogy still applies. You have people who look up to you. Because we're all connected—look no further than the current global crisis—the way you live your life shapes the way other people live theirs.

This poses one of the underlying mysteries of this book:

If we don't set out to live the unlived life, then how come the majority of us arrive at this unintended destination?

Or to echo inspiration from Thoreau, why do most people "live lives of quiet desperation and die with their song still inside them?"

The answer is simpler than you might think.

It's because they got hacked!

Hacked?

But Carl Jung never held a smartphone, and he certainly didn't have access to a computer, you might be thinking.

I didn't believe it, either, but then I saw the trend. And once my eyes were opened, I found evidence every day. I observed a world getting hacked without even knowing.

Need another example?

I'm the CEO of a publishing company and have overseen well over a thousand people start the book-writing process. These aspiring authors tell me it's their burning desire to get published, some of them with hot, stinging tears rolling down their cheek. Finishing a book is their dream, and maybe it has been for several decades.

Then, a few months later, I hear from many of them again. These emerging authors have the tools, the bandwidth, and the ability. We even provide them with a step-by-step process to accomplish their "burning desire." But when it comes time to do their dream, many of them experience little progress. It may be *novel* to toss around obstacles like writer's block, but everybody knows that's not the real issue.

The truth is, they got hacked too!

It's a familiar story with the person who wants to lose weight, learn a language, or start an herb garden. These dreamers have the best intentions, but they get sidelined in the midst of their doing. Blame it on the weather, the economy, or the inventor of corn chips and salsa—but that's not the real culprit.

Chalk it up to what it truly was—another Hack Attack.

What about you? Can you relate? If so, don't believe the lie—that you're just not a "finisher." It might be easier to swallow such excuses, but maybe you're not to blame. Maybe someone or something hacked you too.

If you want to close the space between your dreaming and doing, then you need the secret weapon of all super-achievers— what I've defined as Unhackability.

This message is for all those who detest the unlived life as much as I do. It's for those who've lost people with their song still inside them and felt the unbearable weight at their funerals. If you've ever driven away from a graveyard and vowed your legacy will be different, then you've come to the right book.

Read the table of contents, and you'll notice there are no chapters in this book, only days. So, this content can be digested one day at a time. Or you may want to read multiple days at a time or perhaps all thirty days at once. It's your life and your choice. Go as fast or as slow as you'd like.

One more tip—Unhackability is similar to an onion. There are many layers. You can skim the surface and still benefit—some. Or you can go deep—peeling back layer after layer—and truly become Unhackable. If this is your desire, then look for the reflective questions and action steps at the end of each day. We call this section "Close Your Gap," the place where the content becomes real.

If you're at a difficult place devoid of belief, then borrow mine. When you get to the end of this book, you'll see why.

And now, it's time to become Unhackable. Take your first step by completing the free Unhackability Assessment© on the next page. Besides learning more about yourself, you'll also receive your unique Unhackability score.

You've been made for more and—referencing a scene from the *Dead Poet's Society* movie—it's time we hear your barbaric yawp over the roofs of the world.[1]

—Kary Oberbrunner

THE UNHACKABILITY ASSESSMENT

The Unhackability Assessment© is the first step for helping you discover how to:

- Identify areas where your dreams are getting hacked
- Leverage your unique strengths
- Implement your best ideas
- Tap into your hidden ability for superhuman focus
- Become 500% more productive in work and life

Visit UnhackableBook.com to take the free assessment and receive your baseline Unhackability score.

UNHACKABILITY
ASSESSMENT

UnhackableBook.com

INTRODUCTION

Heart racing and adrenaline pumping, I bolted upright in my bed. Although it was dark, I saw the outline of my wife lying next to me, still sound asleep. Disoriented and confused, I rubbed my forehead and felt the heat.

It was the middle of the night on the eve of October 8, 2014, and I'd just awakened from a dream. After a few moments of heavy breathing, I realized where I was, laid back down, and drifted off to sleep again. The next day, I found my phone, started a note, and quickly tapped out as much as I could remember—twelve lines of text, to be exact.

Those twelve lines would forever alter my life.

MY INTRO TO HACKING

I named the note *Elixir Project*. The premise of my dream was how humans were in danger of getting hacked and in a way no one imagined. Although it began with a single thought, two years later, it morphed into a young adult near-future novel I published in 2016.

For a guy who writes business books, authoring a fiction book—much less one with dystopian overtones geared for teens—was like transforming a TED talk into a middle school assembly speech. When I shared the initial idea with my colleagues, many of them advised against it—warning that it might leave a serious stain on my publishing career. They also reminded me of the fact that I knew nothing about science fiction, hackers, or teen novels.

They had a point.

I knew their caution was motivated by kindness, not cruelty. Besides, I agreed with them. I was the least likely candidate to write that book. I didn't even *read* fiction—much less write it. Plus, my graduate and post-graduate degrees had nothing to do with science or technology. And to top it off, our three kids were still in elementary school—far from being teenagers.

Still, I couldn't shake the idea. And despite trying to abandon it for several months, something kept drawing me back to it. To quote Morpheus from *The Matrix*—one of the few science fiction movies I actually had seen—it was like a "splinter in my mind," and the only way to remove it was to write it.

So, with a healthy dose of trepidation, I finally followed author Steven Pressfield's exhortation and punched Resistance in the face. On an average Tuesday, I enrolled in an online fiction-writing course.

It was designed as a self-study course, and I blazed a trail into this foreign genre solo, feeling like a space traveler exploring a distant planet. Looking back, I see that description is fairly accurate. My research required me to venture into an underworld known as the dark web.

Many days, it felt like I had stumbled into a different universe. I discovered new terms like "cyber espionage" and "Silk Road." I met new players like Dread Pirate Roberts and The Onion Router. I consumed new alarming content like Marc Goodman's *Future Crimes* and encouraging content such as Peter Diamandis' *Abundance Insider*.

I even encountered new websites that provided cyber-attack statistics, breaking them down into categories including cyber-crime, hacktivism, and cyber warfare.

In a way, that little dream back in October 2014 woke me up to a brand-new world. Like most people, up until that point, I was simply asleep to the digital conspiracy growing in the shadows yet silently infecting us all.

A JOURNEY INTO AWARENESS

When I first started writing my fiction book, I thought it would end where it began—with a completed young adult novel. However, once I dug deeper, I realized this rabbit hole was much deeper than I ever imagined.

So, for the next six years, I dove headfirst into a multi-disciplinary exploration of neurobiology, productivity, art, science, technology, athletics, military, and business. I mined the experts and the classics. The lines quickly blurred between science fiction and science fact. Eventually, missing pieces fell into place, and a paradigm emerged that I'll share now and expound upon later. I call it the Unhackable Circle©, and it's comprised of three components: Idea, Focus, Flow.

What I found changed the way I saw everything. It put words to the angst I'd felt for quite some time. Unable to keep quiet, I shared my findings with our global community—the Igniting Souls Tribe.

Like hard-wired entrepreneurs, they echoed my enthusiasm and test-drove the model in their own contexts. These men and women represented a wide variety of demographics and psychographics. They came from dozens of countries and nearly every sector of society—boomers to millennials, white-collar to blue-collar. Regardless of their background, their results were as riveting as mine.

In a short while, you'll hear their stories in their words. Although the details differ, the plotline sounds eerily familiar. Every single person awoke to the truth—that they too had been hacked.

This brings us to the goal of the book—a simple goal, actually.

Like them, I believe you were created to become Unhackable.

And the rest of this book will show you how to do that—how to create flawless ideas, leverage superhuman focus, and achieve optimal human performance through flow.

Get ready for The Unveiling.

UNHACKABILITY
ASSESSMENT

If you haven't already completed the free Unhackability Assessment©, please do so now.

You'll thank me in the end.

Besides learning more about yourself, you'll also receive your unique Unhackability score.

UnhackableBook.com

PART 1

UNVEILING

DAY 1

STORY:
Write Your Story

Live the story you want to tell.

—Unknown

Yesterday, I walked down the tan carpeted stairs into our finished basement. Since it was an early Saturday morning, my wife and kids were still asleep. I planned on riding on my indoor bike while listening to an audiobook.

I turned left and stood perplexed. Instead of a plain white door, I saw pink streamers in tight coils. Across the front of the door, bright-colored signs screamed their warnings:

Only Girls Allowed!

Kid Zone Inside

Enter at Your Own Risk

Password Required

Since I didn't know the password, I entered cautiously—waltzing through the maze of obstacles back to my bicycle. I braced myself for any traps they'd set for trespassers. I had forgotten my two daughters planned on spending most of their Saturday in their newly furnished "Kid Zone." Cardboard, markers, and stuffed animals transformed this dull space into a zoo, or spaceship, or whatever else they imagined.

REMEMBER THE SIMPLE LIFE?

Let's be honest. Life was simpler when we were kids.

We had clarity—at least about our dreams. On ordinary afternoons, our imaginations became our reality. But then, we grew up and became adults, and everything changed. Now, we have full inboxes, packed calendars, global headlines, and thin margins.

Clearly, we're no longer in charge.

Someone or something else is running our lives. No one needs to remind us because we feel it every day. Life is happening to us, not the other way around. So, we operate on autopilot since it's easier—at least that's what we tell ourselves when we have a rare moment to think. But we don't have time to think because we've settled for a life by default rather than by design.

We're distracted from our most important work. And unfortunately, a life of distractions will never produce a life of meaning.

Sure, we have ideas, but up until now, we've been unable to implement most of them. Our unfulfilled dreams weigh heavy, like a thick coat drenched by an uninvited downpour. Although we may attribute our impotence to a variety of factors—busyness, interruptions, burnout—it's more serious than all of these combined.

Simply put, the inability to implement our ideas is a result of being hacked.

FIRST, THE BAD NEWS

Although I'm an optimist, I must warn you about an impending danger. You're smack dab in the middle of a war, and you're probably not even aware of it.

I'm not a fan of hype or hyperbole. But the truth is that you're minutes away from getting hacked, perhaps before you even finish this page.

Strike that.

You could be getting hacked at this moment—in real time. I'm not referring to your computer, phone, or bank account. Those types of hacks can be remedied. The hack I'm referring to is costlier than all of those combined.

I'm referring to your brain.

Have you ever had an amazing idea? If you're like the bulk of the population, you started out excited, ready to make your dream come true. But then, something happened. Chances are you and your idea got sidelined somewhere along the way.

Maybe you were distracted, or perhaps you simply lost focus? If you've experienced this, then you're not alone.

Just as phones and computers get hacked, people get hacked too. Hacking simply means someone or something gained unauthorized access to a system or computer. Although we often think of electronic devices getting hacked, humans become hacked as well. Our bodies are composed of *systems* (respiratory, circulatory, digestive, and immune, to name a few), and our brains operate like *supercomputers*.

Navigating our noisy world long enough to accomplish our daily tasks—much less do our dreams—is nearly impossible, especially these days. The odds are clearly stacked against us, and temptations lurk less than an arm's length away:

- **Smartphones are hacking us**: Statistics vary, but according to a study performed by dscout, on average people touch their phones 2,617 times a day.[2] (Heavy users touch 5,427 times.) More than half of these sessions last less than thirty seconds and are spread throughout the day.

- **Multitasking is hacking us**: Multitasking is a myth. The brain can only do one cognitive activity at a time. Multitasking, more properly understood as switch-tasking, decreases productivity by up to 40%. According to Forbes, "Multitasking with electronic media caused a greater decrease in IQ than smoking pot."[3]

- **Social media is hacking us**: Americans spend more than two hours a day on social media, with most of that time in small, unplanned bits of time that interrupt their work or other scheduled activities.

- **Streaming videos are hacking us**: According to ReelnReel, 11 billion hours are spent watching videos on Netflix every month.[4]

- **Advertisements are hacking us**: *The New York Times* reveals the average person sees 5,000 ads a day.[5]

- **Decision fatigue is hacking us:** Researchers at Cornell University discovered the average person makes 226.7 food decisions a day.[6] This number doesn't take into account the 35,000 other decisions the average person makes on a daily basis. This excessive amount depletes our energy and diverts our focus.

Brace yourself. We haven't seen anything yet. Thanks to advances in science and technology, the amount of information doubles every twelve hours. Fear of missing out (FOMO) legitimately infects young and old alike, driving us to remain digitally connected every waking moment.

But have we stopped to ask the cost?

Cutting-edge wearables and ingestibles raise the stakes in real time. And although innovation isn't the enemy, unless we employ a solution, we'll soon become a generation of casualties.

THEY WANT AN ASSET CALLED ATTENTION

Welcome to the Attention Economy—where *you* are the product. In this digital landscape, they keep score with eyeballs and eardrums. Focus is everything, and they're willing to fight for yours. They no longer track the cash. That's too far down the line. They know what precedes the purchasing decision. *Your attention.*

We call it *paying* attention for a reason. Businesses, politicians, and even non-profits know your thoughts are worth a price, and they'll do almost anything to gain market share. Social media keeps score with likes, views, shares, subscribers, and comments.

The metrics may differ, but the strategy doesn't. If *they* can divert or distract you, they win. If they can sideline or sabotage your plans, they succeed.

It's connected to the Altered States Economy (how we use various sources to shift our state of mind), and according to research done by Steven Kotler and Jamie Wheal in *Stealing Fire*, it represents four trillion dollars. Ironically, we're choosing to get hacked, and we're footing the bill for it.

But getting hacked comes with a price more costly than dollars and cents. By adopting roles as consumers rather than creators, we fail to embody our divine destiny. Visit your email inbox for proof. In it, you'll discover everyone else's agenda for your life—the next virtual meeting you must attend, the next project you must complete, and the next practice you must schedule, not to mention the unending invitations and obligations you must consider.

Thankfully, there is a better way and a better world. As I mentioned in the Introduction, through this multi-disciplinary exploration of neurobiology, productivity, art, science, technology, athletics, military, and business, you'll soon discover the unmistakable elixir behind all idea achievement. Not just for elite performers, this secret weapon is now available to aspiring super-achievers everywhere.

Whoever said, "Ideas can change the world" wasn't correct. Only *implemented* ideas can. The difference between these two statements is a gap as wide as the universe itself. *Unhackable* reveals the proven process to closing that gap—the gap between dreaming and doing.

GET READY FOR THE GOOD NEWS

Becoming Unhackable has serious advantages. Here are four of the most common benefits we've seen in people who've applied the model:

(1) **Productivity**: Unhackable people are more productive.

> Without even realizing it, the past few days I've been getting in the zone. I've gotten a ton of work done with book two, the house is clean and organized, and I'm on top of two other projects that would have normally overwhelmed me. My productivity has sky-rocketed, and it's only day three.
>
> —Nanette O'Neal, author and editor

> I've been in flow all this week, and I have accomplished so much. I can't believe it.
>
> —Tanisha Williams, former schoolteacher

(2) **Fulfillment**: Unhackable people are more fulfilled.

> I am 86 years old and I have never been more fully alive than now.
>
> —Pat Gano, retired

At first, I cried because I realized all the times I had been hacked … and that being hacked kept me from my true potential. But then, my heart was full of joy because I am now doing what I'm intended to do.

—Scott Eckelberg, speaker

(3) **Focus:** Unhackable people are more focused.

Mind blown by this process! The daily method is working. My clarity is growing stronger. Had I not let go of the process I was stuck in and applied this proven method, I fear what would have never been.

—Wendy A. Gentry, college professor

(4) **Margin:** Unhackable people experience more margin.

I took action and unsubscribed from half of my emails lists to reduce distractions. I removed 12 of 24 Facebook groups, 16 of 31 LinkedIn groups, three of five membership sites, and 105 of 151 email lists. I feel free!

—Jeffrey Kramer, city engineer

This is soul-searching, soul-liberating stuff. I have spent the last month walking away from those things that are not in alignment with my Boon. I needed this experience to anchor me.

—Barbara Littles, lawyer

THE SCIENCE BEHIND THE STORIES

These four benefits—productivity, fulfillment, focus, and margin—are only the beginning. You'll sink your teeth into many more along the way.

Before we unpack the science behind Unhackability, let's take a peek at Disney. Maybe Walt was on to something. On July 17, 1955, he declared the motto of Disneyland as "The Happiest Place on Earth." Over the years, the company adopted the slogan "The Place Where Dreams Come True."

So, which is it—the happiest place on earth or the place where dreams come true?

According to biochemistry and psychology, it's both!

In his article titled "Goal Progress and Happiness" in *Psychology Today*, Timothy A. Pychyl, PhD, says—

> The successful pursuit of meaningful goals plays an important role in the development and maintenance of our psychological well-being. To the extent that we're making progress on our goals, we're happier emotionally and more satisfied with our lives.

Translation?

Happiness is the byproduct when we live our dreams and accomplish our goals. But before we break out the champagne and celebrate, consider the alternative. Unhappiness is the byproduct when we get hacked and fail to implement our ideas.

Shawn Achor, Harvard-trained researcher and best-selling author of *The Happiness Advantage,* explains why. "Happiness isn't just about feeling good, it's about the joy we feel while striving after our potential."

A deeper look reveals that each of us is hard-wired to dream and do. This includes big dreams like building a house, completing a degree, or finishing a screenplay. But it also includes small dreams like exercising, organizing your garage, or getting your assignment completed on time.

When you know your daily goals and make progress toward them, you feel good. But when you're hacked, you experience mental and emotional anguish. If getting hacked becomes a pattern, you'll drift toward depression, emotional eating, or other unhealthy coping mechanisms.

Try and deny it, but your DNA doesn't lie.

Although we'll explore examples from a variety of disciplines, let's start with the Judeo-Christian creation story. Genesis 1:3 says, "God said, 'Let there be light,' and there was light."

God didn't say, "Let there be light," and then get distracted playing Xbox or get sucked into binge-watching the latest series. Instead, we see a zero gap between ideation and implementation. In other words, God didn't get hacked.

IDEATION  IMPLEMENTATION

DIVINE DESTINY

Unfortunately, we humans get hacked all the time. We fail to implement our ideas. Our new normal means we go from ideation to frustration or stagnation. Instead of embodying our divine destiny, we settle for a depraved reality instead.

IDEATION  STAGNATION

FRUSTRATION

DEPRAVED REALITY

As long as we keep getting sidelined and sabotaged, we'll remain stuck in an endless cycle of angst. Scrolling our latest newsfeed or social media channel won't silence our ache.

We know something isn't quite right.

We hear it in the melody lines of movies and music.

We understand we were meant for more, but we're not sure how to translate that into everyday life.

Only when we revisit the "playground of life" do we discover a significant clue.

A WEIGHTY WORD

I'm the blessed father of three young—but growing—kids.

All I need to do is listen closely to them during playtime, and I'll hear one particular word often. It's the same word my parents used when they were kids. And it's the same word their parents used in their childhood. In fact, it's been passed on through generation after generation for several thousand years.

Abracadabra is made up of three Hebrew words: father, son, spirit.

Linguists label it as the most universally adopted word pronounced in other languages without the need for translation.

We used the word without even knowing what it meant. Most often, we said it when we wanted to make something magical happen.

Abracadabra means "I create as I speak." And it's literally translated, "It came to pass as it was spoken."

Even as children, we longed to experience a zero gap between ideation and implementation. We wanted to speak into existence the thoughts dominating our minds and the dreams inhabiting our hearts.

But maybe abracadabra was never intended to be only make-believe.

IS IT TIME FOR A NEW STORY?

Kids of all ages love stories. In the beginning of time, the oral tradition was how we remembered our past, understood our present, and prepared for our future.

Today, we tell stories to help us process our place in this world. We spin thousands of micro-stories every day. We'll say things like:

- You don't deserve that *because* …

- You should let someone else speak first *because* …

- Nobody values your opinion *because* …

- You aren't one of those people *because* …

- You were never good at that *because* …

- You didn't really want it anyways *because* …

- No one ever listens to you *because* …

Stories bring context and meaning to the moment. Unfortunately, these same stories often hold us back. They create prison bars around what's possible.

In the conversation about becoming Unhackable, it's easy to sabotage ourselves before we even start. If we're not careful, we'll bring an old story right along with us. We'll say things like:

- You'll never implement your idea *because* …

- You always get distracted *because* …

- You've never been good at staying focused *because* …

- You've always quit before achieving your goals *because* …

- You'll never do your dream *because* …

- You'll always get hacked *because* …

The story we tell ourselves *now* shapes our reality *later*. After coaching thousands of people over the past two decades,

I've realized that we humans tend to do something odd. *We argue for things we don't want.*

In one breath, we'll say how we want to become more productive and focused. We'll fantasize over having greater fulfillment and margin in our lives.

Then, in the next breath, we'll say things like, "Yeah, but you don't understand …" We'll spend exorbitant amounts of time and energy trying to convince ourselves why it can't happen for us.

The truth is we don't get what we want—*we get what we argue for.* Here's why. The reason is found in the old adage, "Where your focus goes, your energy flows." When we focus on why it won't work or how it can't happen to us, we waste energy and emotion betting against our desires. Essentially, we stack the deck against ourselves by directing our creative power toward unproductive action.

Trying to quit cold turkey won't stop the cycle. Rather than hoping to drop the bad habit, we should replace it with a good one instead. This yields productive action.

We'll close this first day with a simple yet powerful exercise that will give you the ability to create a new story.

UP UNTIL NOW

Denying your old story is an exercise in futility. It feels inauthentic to ignore your personal history, like you're trying to swallow a lie. So rather than attempting to forget your past, create the space for a new future instead.

One of my mentors taught me three powerful words that make this possible: *up until now.* It won't feel impressive in this moment, but use it in real time, and you'll feel the magic. The next time you tell yourself an undesirable story, use *up until now* as a preface. For example:

- *Up until now*, I've never implemented my idea …

- *Up until now*, I've always gotten distracted ...

- *Up until now*, I've never been good at staying focused ...

- *Up until now*, I've always quit before achieving my goals ...

- *Up until now*, I've never done my dream ...

- *Up until now*, I've always gotten hacked ...

These three words will allow you to change your story rather than regurgitating the old one subconsciously swimming in your head. In a way, it's a weapon to ward off the self-sabotaging thinking that's hacked you in the past.

Up until now gives you permission to write a new story instead. Think of it as your first act of co-creation, a legitimate effort to return to your childhood days. You'll sink your teeth into a simpler version of life once again. In this world, you'll

- create ideas and implement them effectively

- architect your attention and invest in the things important to you

- find and utilize the needed resources to accomplish your dream

- exponentially increase your impact upon the world

- organize your life around flow—where you feel your best and perform your best

As I mentioned in my personal note to you at the beginning of this book, at the end of each day, I'll provide you with one clear action step. For example, today, I'm challenging you to write your story. By doing this, you give yourself permission to create a new future. Take this action, and you'll start closing the gap between dreaming and doing. Most importantly, you'll discover how to become Unhackable.

Abracadabra is closer than you think.

CLOSE YOUR GAP DAY 1: WRITE YOUR STORY

1. In the past, what story have you told yourself to explain why you didn't achieve your goals? Please list as many micro-stories as possible via bullet points.

   For example:

   - I didn't have the resources I needed ...

   - I didn't have people who supported me ...

   - I didn't have the necessary experience ...

2. Does this past story serve your future dream?

3. Go back to your micro-stories above and change the beginning. Insert the words "up until now."

For example:

- *Up until now* ... I didn't have the resources I needed.

- *Up until now* ... I didn't have people who supported me.

- *Up until now* ... I didn't have the necessary experience.

4. Now, write your new story. Rather than focusing on what you don't have, write out what you want instead. Don't write in the future tense—*I will have* or *I will be*. Instead, write in the present tense—*I have* or *I am*.

DAY 2

DESIRE:
Pick Your Boon

*Don't ask yourself what the world needs. Ask yourself what
makes you come alive, because what the world needs
is people who have come alive.*

—Howard Thurman

We've all met them—the ultra-serious *Star Wars* fan—
so hardcore they don't even need a nickname like
Star Trek fans (Trekkies). I researched this point
to make sure they're truly nickname-less. After checking the
Jedi Council Forums, I can confirm this fact with certainty.[7]
(I didn't want to offend them and get sliced in two with a
lightsaber, now an official sport in France.[8])

Film director George Lucas had no idea his 1977 exper-
iment would create such a cult following. Truth is, it almost
didn't—that is, until he integrated a Boon within the storyline.

BACKSTORY OF THE BOON

If you're unfamiliar with the concept of a Boon, it's the bedrock of Joseph Campbell's seminal book, *The Hero with a Thousand Faces,* and therefore—as fate would have it—*Star Wars* too. (Buckle up. A brief history lesson about Boons will shed a ton of clarity about how to become Unhackable.)

George Lucas credits Joseph Campbell's work as a major influence upon his movies. He had already written two drafts of *Star Wars* when he rediscovered Campbell's book in 1975 (having read it years before in college). This blueprint for the "Hero's Journey" gave Lucas the focus he needed to draw his sprawling imaginary universe into a single story.[9]

The Hero's Journey is a way of understanding the world. The rationale is simple. Myths from every culture use the same basic elementary ideas, or as Carl Jung named them—archetypes. According to Jung, every person possesses the basic subconscious model of what a hero is, or a mentor, or a quest. It's as if we're all born with an innate sense. This is why people who don't even speak the same language can still enjoy the same stories—the Harry Potter books, for example.

Campbell took this idea of archetypes further and named these different parts that make up the story pattern. Also known as the monomyth, together, these parts describe the journey every hero must take to experience true transformation.

The pattern goes something like this. A hero starts in the ordinary world, then he or she receives a call to enter an unusual world of strange powers and events (a call to adventure).

If the hero accepts the call to enter this world, the hero must face several tasks (a road of trials), perhaps alone or with assistance. At its most intense, the hero encounters a severe challenge, often with help earned along the journey. If the hero survives, he or she may achieve a great gift (the goal, or Boon), which often results in the discovery of important self-knowledge.

The hero must then decide whether to return with this Boon (the return to the ordinary world), often facing challenges along the way. If the hero is successful in returning, the Boon or gift may be used to improve the world (the application of the Boon). This final phase completes the Hero's Journey.

Most movies, stories, and plays follow this story arc.

Unpacking the Hero's Journey

Although these components can be understood in story form, breaking them down into steps provides additional clarity. Not all myths contain every step, and other myths rearrange the order, but most follow this pattern:

Part 1: Departure

1. The Call to Adventure
2. Refusal of the Call
3. Supernatural Aid
4. Crossing the First Threshold
5. The Belly of the Whale

Part 2: Initiation

6. The Road of Trials
7. The Meeting with the Goddess
8. Temptation Away from the True Path
9. Atonement with the Father
10. Apotheosis (Becoming God-Like)
11. **The Ultimate Boon**

Part 3: Return

12. Refusal of the Return

13. The Magic Flight

14. Rescue from Without

15. Crossing the Return Threshold

16. Master of the Two Worlds

17. Freedom to Live

We witness this Hero's Journey in the movies we watch, the books we read, and even the lives we live. Arguably, the Boon is the most critical component. It's why the hero accepts the journey in the first place, though often it's not entirely clear what the Boon is in the beginning. All the previous steps serve to prepare and purify the person for this step. In many myths, the Boon is something transcendent like the elixir of life, a plant that supplies immortality, or the Holy Grail.

If you are one of those loyal *Star Wars* superfans, you'll appreciate how George Lucas integrated each component of the Hero's Journey throughout his films:

Part 1: Departure

1. Princess Leia's message = *The Call to Adventure*

2. Must help with the harvest = *Refusal of the Call*

3. Obi-Wan rescues Luke from the sand people = *Supernatural Aid*

4. Escaping Tatooine = *Crossing the First Threshold*

5. Trash compactor = *The Belly of the Whale*

Part 2: Initiation

6. Lightsaber practice = *The Road of Trials*

7. Princess Leia = *The Meeting with the Goddess*

8. Luke is tempted by the Dark Side = *Temptation Away from the True Path*

9. Darth Vader and Luke reconcile = *Atonement with the Father*

10. Luke becomes a Jedi = *Apotheosis (becoming God-Like)*

11. **Death Star destroyed = *The Ultimate Boon***

Part 3: Return

12. Luke wants to stay to avenge Obi-Wan = *Refusal of the Return*

13. Millennium Falcon = *The Magic Flight*

14. Han saves Luke from Darth Vader = *Rescue from Without*

15. Millennium Falcon destroys pursuing TIE fighters = *Crossing the Return Threshold*

16. Victory Ceremony = *Master of the Two Worlds*

17. Rebellion is victorious over Empire = *Freedom to Live*

Notice component number eleven—the destruction of the Death Star. If Luke failed to achieve this step—his ultimate Boon—the entire journey would have been fruitless. Evil would triumph, and good would perish.

The stakes are also high with *The Lord of the Rings* and *The Matrix*. (Visit UnhackableBook.com/free to see a breakdown of how these respective films integrate the Hero's Journey and the ultimate Boon.)

It's no different with your life. You have an ultimate Boon too. You've felt the call to adventure, and perhaps—*up until now*—you've even refused that call. But it's time to tap into your supernatural aid. It's time to become Unhackable. And make no mistake, because your life isn't make-believe, the stakes are even higher.

RECOVER YOUR BOON

You'd think most of us would be able to articulate what our Boon is, but this is rarely the case. Boons are big because they represent your deepest desire, your greatest ache, your truest longing.

As adults, most of us are disconnected from our heart's desire. Maybe at some point, we knew. But we've forgotten somewhere along the way.

Desire is an interesting word. It literally means to give birth. Finding this desire is more about recovery than discovery. I think back to my life. As a kid, I loved writing stories. Rummaging through a memory box the other day, I found a yellow robot I must have traced and cut out in first grade. On the other side of that robot, I wrote a simple story—five paragraphs long—about a boy, Mike, and his robot, Mighty.

As the years ticked off and I entered middle school, I forgot about writing. Maybe I was too caught up trying to be cool? Whatever the reason, I pursued several other hobbies before rediscovering my love for writing in my early twenties. Since then, I've cultivated this passion.

What about you? What's emerging from your soul? This question may be simple, as easy as naming your favorite color or admitting your favorite song. Or it may be unknown and complex, a foreign feeling—like meeting a mysterious stranger on a chance encounter in an unfamiliar city.

Regardless, as you keep digging into Unhackability, mark my words, you will discover clarity. It's the unavoidable byproduct. Sure, clarity may not come all at once—for many, it comes in waves, one imperfect action at a time. But Boons always surface for those willing to do the work. It's time to answer your call, once and for all, and close your gap.

CLOSE YOUR GAP DAY 2: PICK YOUR BOON

1. What is your deepest desire, your greatest ache, your truest longing? Editing isn't allowed, and don't focus on being correct either. In all this, don't aim for perfection. Nobody sees his or her Boon perfectly in the beginning—just like Luke from *Star Wars*, Frodo from *The Lord of the Rings*, Neo from *The Matrix*, and Katniss Everdeen from *Hunger Games*. Clarity comes as you take action. Picking your Boon is like emerging out of a fog. Embrace the paradox: the clouds lift when you move toward your desire.

2. Still need a little more help picking your Boon? My friend Mike Kim says it another way. He asks his clients, "What pisses you off? What breaks your heart? What's the big problem you're trying to solve?" Answer these questions openly and honestly with the first thing that pops in your mind. (If you're ambitious, visit UnhackableBook.com/free to access 80+ more questions that will help you pick your Boon.)

DAY 3

CULPRIT:
Identify Your Culprit

The impediment to action advances action.
What stands in the way becomes the way.

—Marcus Aurelius

Eighty minutes.

That's how long you need to watch the movie *Jaws* before you actually *see* the infamous shark. Some film critics attribute Steven Spielberg's strategy for delaying the identity of the antagonist as pure genius. Other critics claim it was because he lacked the budget and time to produce a gigantic mechanical shark on schedule. Still others believe the large metal monster wouldn't cooperate and sank to the bottom of the ocean before they could rebuild a replacement. Regardless of the rationale, his strategy of invoking terror worked, evidenced by audiences' frightened screams for decades to come.

Although we didn't see the shark for an hour, twenty minutes into the film, we saw the damage and death it produced.

And we heard the same haunting musical score every time the shark stalked its prey through the murky waters.

Psychologists agree that we fear what we *can't* see even more than what we *can* see. Consider the scary times of 2020—a virus we couldn't see. Or think even further back to the terrorist attacks of September 11, 2001—initiated by an "invisible" enemy.

In both situations, for many people, their imaginations took over because they confronted a nameless or faceless threat. When we can't label the culprit, we can't *control* the culprit. Our vulnerability produces an unsettling feeling and gives our mind permission to fill in the blanks. This mental anguish produces psychological pain, often much more damaging than any physical pain. This prison of the mind holds us hostage, and we start believing escape is no longer possible.

Thankfully, the opposite is true too. When we unmask our adversary, we immediately regain a sense of control. We know who or what threatens us and how we can defeat it. By discovering its weakness, we gain an edge that helps us outwit our opponent and ultimately defeat it.

The first step in winning this war is identifying the culprit. It was true for the town in *Jaws*, and it's true for you in your Hero's Journey.

UNDERSTANDING YOUR ADVERSARY

Let's begin by exploring the definition of a culprit. The Merriam-Webster Dictionary says it's "one accused of or charged with a crime."[10]

The truth is you have an enemy. You've known this your entire life. Whenever you dream of what's possible and set out to achieve it, you feel the opposition bearing down upon you. Although you were created to be Unhackable, with a zero gap between your dreaming and doing, this is not your reality.

Sometimes it feels like you're blindsided from out of nowhere. Life simply shows up with its fair share of trials:

unexpected bills, undesired conflicts, and uninvited problems. Other times, you lack the margin and energy to do what you'd like. When you finally find the time, you're so tired and stressed you lack the creativity and drive to work on your dream.

If you're like most people with a dream, you started out excited—ready to implement your idea. But then, opposition came from out of nowhere. It's easy to attribute your lack of implementation to distractions or loss of focus. The brutal truth is that you got hacked.

Sounds mighty similar to a sci-fi movie—except that it's not. Remember our definition a hack—when someone or something gains unauthorized access to a system or computer. This means anytime you've been diverted from your dream, you've been hacked.

The average person spends a total of five hours a day browsing the web and using apps. This equates to around a third of the time we are awake, and it's twice as much as we think we spend. Researchers have found that smartphone use is typically confined to short bursts with more than half of uses lasting less than thirty seconds. This means people experience distracted work far more regularly than what Georgetown University Professor Cal Newport calls "deep work."

There's a reason. In a 2009 paper titled "Why Is It So Hard to Do My Work?" by Sophie Leroy, a business school professor at the University of Minnesota reveals that multitasking produces "attention residue" or the inability to transition tasks effectively.[11] This, in turn, saps mental energy, ruins concentration, and reduces overall productivity. The majority of us are ill-equipped to successfully navigate this overstimulated new world.

NOW FOR THE GOOD NEWS

Your adversary can be defeated with a little introspection and truth-telling.

Remember Day 2 when you picked your Boon? Although you might not have articulated it perfectly, you took your first step out of the fog and wrote down some of your thoughts. This Boon represents your Future Expectations.

Look at the chart below. On the right side, jot down a few of these thoughts about your Boon—your deepest desire, your greatest ache, your truest longing. Don't worry about flawless clarity. Aim for imperfect action. Remember, clarity only comes with action.

PRESENT EXPERIENCE	HACKED	FUTURE EXPECTATIONS

Once you're done, jump to the left side of the chart. It represents your Present Experience. It's a picture of your old story that has held you back up until now. In Day 1, you articulated this story. Jot down a few phrases that reflect this old story. It might be "not enough" or "failure." Whatever your past limitations have been, list them on the chart.

The gap between your Future Expectations and your Present Experience represents who or what is hacking you. Without consciously thinking about it, in the center column above, make a quick list of all the people or things getting in your way and creating space between you and your Boon.

Once you've completed the center column, review your list. Do you see any patterns in these hacks? Write down some of your observations below:

Did certain names keep showing up? What about particular locations or activities?

When I did this activity many years ago, long before I became an entrepreneur, I noticed a revealing trend. In the middle column, I listed my boss, my director, and my limited time due to my job description. If you'd asked me what my biggest hack was back then, I would have enthusiastically pointed the finger at other people and circumstances. No wonder I felt so powerless. I couldn't control my boss, my director, or my job description. Still, I grumbled and complained. Talk about an unproductive period! All that negativity sucked away my time and energy—not to mention my life too.

Blaming our hacks on other people and things is easy to do. But the reality is, we're in control of our day jobs, our smartphones, our time, and our resources. Blaming others, making excuses, and living in denial doesn't solve the problem; it only prolongs the pain.

In this state of mind, we view ourselves as victims who are powerless. We become reactive, and the world simply *happens* to us. In a way, we lie in BED (blame, excuses, denial).

V
I
C
T
I
M

B   Blame
E   Excuses
D   Denial

I know this place quite well. Although I wouldn't admit it then, looking back now, I recognize I lived my life from a victim mindset. Sure, other people or things might have been hacking me, but I allowed it.

Thankfully, I didn't stay there forever. When my mindset changed, so did my life.

By adopting a victor mindset, I moved forward into my future by leveraging my OAR (ownership, accountability, responsibility). You can too. In this place, we become proactive again by *happening* to the world.

V I C T O R	O	Ownership
	A	Accountability
	R	Responsibility

CLOSE YOUR GAP DAY 3: IDENTIFY YOUR CULPRIT

It's time to identify the culprit hacking you. Remember the definition: "A culprit is one accused of or charged with a crime." Although none of us wakes up intending to get hacked, we're responsible for allowing ourselves to be hacked. This admission is the first step to massive transformation. Until we do this, we're stuck in a cycle of unproductive blame-shifting.

Do you admit to being the culprit? If so, you're close to a major breakthrough. Lasting change means you commit to doing these four things:

1. Become a proactive victor.

2. Take ownership of your pattern for getting hacked.

3. Become accountable for your hacking problem.

4. Embrace your responsibility for the need to change.

You might wonder if you have another option. You always have a choice. You can remain safe and stuck by denying your role as the culprit.

If so, this means you will do the following:

1. Stay a reactive victim.

2. Continue blaming other people and things.

3. Keep on making excuses for why you're getting hacked.

4. Live in denial about the fact that you're getting hacked.

You can't take another step in your Hero's Journey until you make a choice.

- Neo had to choose between the red pill or the blue pill.

- Frodo had to choose to take the One Ring or stay in the Shire.

- Luke Skywalker had to choose to answer Leia's plea or remain a farm boy.

- Katniss had to choose the Hunger Games or watch her sister, Prim, lose her life.

- You have to choose to admit or deny the role of the culprit hacking you.

The choice you make will make you. Remember, the truth will set you free. Pick one response below, and be honest.

☐ I am the culprit. I am responsible for getting hacked.

☐ I am NOT the culprit. I am NOT responsible for getting hacked.

DAY 4

CONSPIRACY:
Confront Your Conspiracy

*[We] are masters of [our] fates; The fault ... is not in our stars,
but in ourselves, that we are underlings.*

—Shakespeare

Are you in danger of someone hacking your vehicle? Weird question, I know.

Perhaps irrelevant twenty years ago, but today, it's a threat real enough to warrant an entire news episode devoted to the topic. I watched one such episode with my wife, Kelly, awhile back. It exposed a conspiracy unbeknownst to me—the possibility of someone hacking your car while you're driving it.

Since many modern cars are essentially a large computer with four wheels, hacking one is relatively simple. Certain makes and models of cars possess serious vulnerabilities. The television episode was both interesting and alarming.

Although these newscasters knew the vehicle they drove was about to be hacked by an unidentified hacker from a remote computer, when they felt the effects of the actual hack, their responses were similar. They displayed shock, confusion, and bewilderment.

Horns blared.

Windshield wipers sped back and forth.

Accelerators engaged—and kept on engaging until the driver released the wheel, bracing for an impending crash. Fear and panic soon overtook the nervous giggles reverberating in the cabin only seconds before. The newscasters found themselves caught up in a conspiracy far more dangerous than they first imagined.

THE HACK ATTACK

Vehicle hacking may be disconcerting, but it doesn't compare to the fallout of true human hacking. These conspiracies are no laughing matter. Rather, they're a calculated plan to inflict serious harm.

After researching the effects of human hacking, I observed a sophisticated sequence I call the Hack Attack. This conspiracy systematically strips away eight essential components and leaves victims vulnerable and exposed. Take a peek and see if you've suffered one of these attacks.

When life hacks you, you'll feel a loss of

1. Control
2. Clarity
3. Competence
4. Confidence
5. Insight
6. Influence
7. Impact
8. Income

Obviously, it's impossible to close the gap between dreaming and doing when you've lost these eight components. Worse yet, when control, clarity, competence, confidence, insight, influence, impact, and income are stripped away, you make powerful negative declarations about yourself and your resources. Notice the pattern below.

A Hack Attack causes you to say

1. *I am not in charge.* (Loss of control)

2. *I am confused.* (Loss of clarity)

3. *I am not good enough.* (Loss of competence)

4. *I am an imposter.* (Loss of confidence)

5. *I have no vision.* (Loss of insight)

6. *I have no effect on others.* (Loss of influence)

7. *I have no credibility.* (Loss of impact)

8. *I have no currency.* (Loss of income)

Hack Attacks start out externally, but they quickly manifest internally. The four *I am* and *I have* declarations shape how you see yourself and the world around you. Perspective matters, and when it's hacked, everything else is hacked too.

According to Anaïs Nin, "We don't see things the way they are, but the way we are."[12] This is why it's so important for you to confront your conspiracy. If you don't, you'll soon believe two lies:

First lie: I Am Nobody.
Second lie: I Have Nothing.

When this occurs, you're done. You settle for scarcity, not surplus—for lack, not abundance. Thankfully, there's good news. You can stop the Hack Attack before it spreads. Even better, you have the opportunity to launch a counterattack. You can reverse the effects and move closer toward Unhackability.

CLOSE YOUR GAP DAY 4: CONFRONT YOUR CONSPIRACY

It's time to close your gap. Verbalize these eight new declarations about your identity and your resources.

A Hack Counterattack empowers you to say:

1. *I am in charge.* (Control)

2. *I am not confused.* (Clarity)

3. *I am good enough.* (Competence)

4. *I am not an imposter.* (Confidence)

5. *I have vision.* (Insight)

6. *I have an effect on others.* (Influence)

7. *I have credibility.* (Impact)

8. *I have currency.* (Income)

The temptation is to rush. Slow down. Go back and say each affirmation about yourself one more time—all eight of them.

These realities will change the way you see yourself and the world around you. Remember, you'll never outperform your self-image, and until you reset your self-image, you'll keep getting hacked. It's time for you to realize two new truths:

First truth: I am somebody.
Second truth: I have something.

Unhackable people are outliers. They know they're somebody with something to offer. They create flawless ideas, leverage superhuman focus, and achieve optimal human performance through flow. You might be one of them.

If so, get ready to pay a price. Everything of value comes with a cost, and Unhackability is no exception.

DAY 5

COST:
Count Your Cost

The best way to predict the future is to create it.

—Atari advertisement

You know the drill.

You're watching a show with a friend, and a commercial comes on with an enthusiastic promoter. Guess what she's selling? Your exact idea—the one you've been thinking of for quite some time.

"She stole my idea!" you blurt out.

Of course you feel angry about the injustice, but you can't do anything about it. What *can* you do when someone else steals an idea that only exists in your mind?

Funny, isn't it? Oftentimes, we don't feel any emotional tie to our idea until we experience someone else taking it.

We don't allow ourselves to feel the pain of missing out on our idea because we never give ourselves permission to imagine what would happen if it actually came true. Since we don't count the cost of what it means to win, we never count the cost of what it means to lose either.

Remaining emotionless is a self-protection strategy. By failing to invest emotion, we remain uncommitted. And as long as we're uncommitted, we don't need to do anything about it—until someone else steals our idea. Then we're suddenly jealous, angry, and upset. The truth is, emotions existed all along. We simply suppressed them until our idea was threatened.

Can you relate?

I can.

FEAR OF COMMITMENT

One of my Boons, writing a young-adult near-future thriller, almost ended before it began. Writing a fiction book and creating a related course would be a major deviation from where I had previously spent my writing career. Investing two full years in this passion project would be risky—personally and professionally.

In the beginning, I experienced fears that come with any idea:

I can't do this.
What if I fail?
I don't have enough experience.
I'm in over my head.

The excuses kept coming. It got worse when friends and colleagues weighed in with their commentary:

Why risk your career?
What will your clients think if it doesn't work out?
Do you even know how to write young-adult fiction?
What makes you believe you're qualified?

You can imagine what happened when I listened to my own chatter, not to mention theirs. I got hacked! My idea stalled, and I froze in fear.

FEAR IS REAL

Refer back to your Boon you identified on Day 2. Be honest. What fears do you have about truly committing to your idea?

Maybe you've shared your idea with others? Maybe you've kept it to yourself? Regardless, know this: negativity will come.

Understandably, I let my *Elixir Project* idea get sidelined and sabotaged for a number of months. True confession—I distracted myself *on purpose*. I thought busyness would help me escape my idea.

Nope. It kept lingering like a piece of corn stuck between my teeth. Not pretty.

Thankfully, I eventually employed a little thinking tool called counting the cost. Rather than focusing on what I *might gain* if I implemented my idea, I flipped my focus. I invested time in thinking about what I *might lose* if I permanently got hacked.

I literally wrote out a letter from a fictitious follower where she told me about the imaginary impact she experienced from reading my book. The letter went something like this:

Dear Kary,

You don't know me, but I read your book, and it changed my life. Let me share the details …

[story of imaginary impact]

Sincerely,
Fictitious Follower

By writing this letter, I counted the cost. I tapped into my *why* for writing *Elixir Project*. This shift made all the difference. Rather than fortifying my fears, I fortified my faith. I emerged emotionally committed to my idea. I now had a name and a face, and whether this person experienced a life change or not depended on whether I implemented my idea or not.

It sounds a little weird, writing a letter from a pretend reader about the imaginary impact *Elixir Project* had on her. The truth is, it's only weird until you realize you can remember your future. You do it all the time—you just might not know it.

Most of us have been taught a lie that memory works in only one direction—backward. We often talk about remembering things from our past.

Who we chose.
What we ate.
When we left.
Where we went.
Why we spoke.

But memory works in two directions—backward and forward. The latest in brain science confirms this:

Imagining the future, for example, involves many of the same brain areas as remembering the past. Your brain activates the hippocampus and medial temporal lobe for all mental time travel—both when you visit the past and go back to the future.[13]

Anytime you worry about something in the future (a speech, test, meeting, etc.), you remember your future. At that moment, you're thinking of something yet to come, and many times, you're even experiencing physiological symptoms connected to the event (sweaty palms, pulse racing, etc.). Anxiety is the result of remembering your future in a negative light.

What if you could imagine your future but in a positive light?

I make this a regular practice. As I imagined my future, I pictured thousands of people whose lives I'd impact by writing

Elixir Project. I may not have known their actual names or seen their actual faces. However, the proof is below. Here are a couple of real people who have shared how *Elixir Project* impacted them in a significant way.

Unhackability should be a daily life choice—Chika U.
Reviewed on June 7, 2019

This book causes you to think about your own life and question things in your life. You begin to wonder about your dreams that have not been realized and why. The book opens your eyes to possibilities. You are faced with a choice to stay the same while Sienna grows and changes or seek to grow and change in your own life. Find out how you are being hacked and become Unhackable.

Couldn't put it down—Selena Marie
Reviewed on July 4, 2018

A mix of science and science fiction, mystery, and excitement, a futuristic taste of a not-so-distant dystopia with a storyline that will put you into the perfect flow. Well worth the lost hours of sleep when you can't put it down.

(I'd be remiss if I didn't share that I received several negative reviews too. Although earlier in my career I didn't enjoy these, now I appreciate it when someone takes the time to tell me their opinion. There's often some truth in their thinking and an opportunity for me to grow.)

The imaginary impact from a fictitious follower gives me the fuel I need to start my project. It also provides me with courage when I reach the "messy middle" and the fire to finish strong.

The funny thing is, one time, I wrote an imaginary impact letter and later received a real one that sounded almost word-for-word the same. To this day, I've never met Kate

Taylor, an entrepreneur from Australia. However, in her own words sent to me six years ago, *Day Job to Dream Job* changed her life:

> There is a man who wrote a book called *Day Job to Dream Job*. I read it because I needed some real ideas on how to get out of working full time in a job I wasn't happy in. It changed my life, and here I am, running my own business. So, thank you, Kary Oberbrunner, for taking the time to put your thoughts down on paper for people like me who just needed some clarity on how to make the jump.

CLOSE YOUR GAP DAY 5: COUNT YOUR COST

Now, it's your turn. I want you to write a letter from a fictitious follower about the imaginary impact your idea created. Be specific. The more detailed you are, the better.

Dear _____,

You don't know me, but your _____ changed my life. Let me share the details ...

[story of imaginary impact]

Sincerely,
Fictitious Follower

This letter is only the beginning. Imagine your idea impacting dozens, hundreds, thousands, millions, or even billions of people.

Ironically, they're all waiting for one thing—you! None of this impact will be experienced if you get hacked. It's time to stop focusing on yourself and your fears. Instead, fortify your faith. Starting now.

PART 2

DAY 6

PROMISE:
Claim your Promise

*Don't promise to live forever. Promise to forever
live while you're alive.*

—Atticus

Welcome to the first component in the Unhackable
Circle©, where we unpack flawless ideas. Some
readers might wonder if such things exist. You be
the judge—only suspend your judgment until we fully examine
all four elements: promise, promotion, progress, and posture.

You'll recognize these elements in every flawless idea
throughout history, including

- John F. Kennedy's "We choose to go to the Moon"
  speech

- Martin Luther King Jr.'s "I Have a Dream" speech

- Jesus Christ's "Sermon on the Mount"

Let's dive into the first element.

FLAWLESS IDEA ANATOMY ELEMENT #1—PROMISE

Promises are powerful. They're the assurance a particular thing will happen. Promises aren't dependent upon circumstances, events, or outcomes.

When you claim a promise, you demand something considered your due. Claiming isn't up for a vote, negotiation, or opinion. Results are irrelevant, and proof is unnecessary. You're simply telling the universe you're ready to assume possession. Claiming means you realize the promise is already yours.

History is full of people who claimed a promise they believed was due them. Here are a few examples to get the juices flowing:

- Rosa Parks *claimed* her seat.

- Henry Ford *claimed* his Model T.

- J.K. Rowling *claimed* her empire.

- Michael Phelps *claimed* his gold (twenty-three and counting).

- Walt Disney *claimed* his theme park.

- The Wright brothers *claimed* their flight.

- Edison *claimed* his light bulb.

- Oprah *claimed* her success.

- Lucille Ball *claimed* her Emmys.

And the list goes on.

Life told all of these people, "No!" many times over. However, they didn't allow external results to extinguish their internal idea. They claimed their promise, and slowly over time, life gave up the fight, tapped out, and relinquished what was rightfully theirs.

YOUR CLAIM TO FAME

So how do you claim a promise?

If you want to claim a big *win*, you need to clarify a big *why*.

You'll probably give up along the way if the idea is only yours. But if you understand your idea was given *through* you, not *to* you, then you understand it's not up to you to open up the heavens and pour down the promises. Your job is simply to maintain belief.

We call this importunity. Regardless of your faith background, it's a little-known law that packs a powerful punch—or in this case, a powerful promise.

In the song "Bullet the Blue Sky," Bono (the frontman of U2) sings, "Jacob wrestled the angel and the angel was overcome." Jacob's life is a great example of importunity. He cashed in on a divinely inspired dream he'd had decades earlier—this *big why* caused him to voice a *big win*. Importunity means incessantly and compulsively making your request known. It's a fierce resolve not to quit until your desire is fulfilled. Jacob wrestled God and wouldn't let go until God blessed him.

It worked!

The angel relented and gave him a new name—*Israel*—the meaning of which signified an even bigger future: *one who wrestled with God and man and overcame.*

REVEALED IN THE RING

We witness importunity whenever a person triumphs against all odds. We observe it when someone with a terminal illness defeats a death sentence and claws back to health. We sense it when an economic downturn threatens a small business that won't surrender even after experiencing punishing blow after punishing blow.

Boxing fans certainly felt importunity in the fight between Buster Douglass and Mike Tyson. If you're not familiar with the context, YouTuber Mateusz M tells the story in a video montage set to Eric Thomas' piercing narration.[14] This two-minute clip will resurrect anyone broken by unbelief:

> You can write everything down if you want to. Be brave enough to write every one of your goals down, but I'm going to tell you something—life's going to hit you in your mouth and you gotta do me a huge favor.
>
> *Your "why" has to be greater than that "knockdown."*
>
> Buster Douglas got knocked out. Nobody ever got knocked out by Mike Tyson and ever got back up. It was almost a ten count. He was stumbling: four, three, two … one … and ding, ding, ding, saved by the bell.
>
> He goes to his corner. The whole world is like, "Yup, that's it." Once he comes back out, that's it. Mike's gonna just hammer him. And exactly that—Mike Tyson came out like, "I got him. I got this kid up against the rope." Listen to me, many of you right now, life's got you up against the rope—you can't give up; you can't give in. …
>
> … And if life's got you backed up, I need you to do what Buster Douglas did. Buster Douglas started fighting back. And the world was shocked!
>
> Goliath has been knocked down. "What happened?"
>
> And they went to Buster Douglas, and they asked Buster Douglas simply like, "What happened?" And Buster Douglas said, "Listen to me, it's real simple. Before my mother died, she told the whole world that I was going to beat Mike Tyson. And two days before the fight, my mother died."

Buster Douglas, he had a decision to make. When his mother died, he can die with his mother, or he made a decision: "I can wake up, and I can live for Mom."

And he knocked Mike Tyson out.

Simply because his "why" was greater than that punch.
His "why" was greater than defeat.
His "why" was greater than his trial and his tribulation.

And I'm telling you, if you don't know what your "why" is and your "why" isn't strong, you're gonna get knocked out every single day.

Your battle will be fierce. This is the reason you need to arm yourself with a *why* big enough to take down your opposition. Your *why* has to be greater than the knockdown.

CLOSE YOUR GAP DAY 6: CLAIM YOUR PROMISE

Clarify Your Why

When I had the idea to write *Elixir Project*, I knew I needed a big why. If my *why* was small, then my *win* would be small, too, and I'd probably lose passion and quit along the way.

Instead, I clarified my why. I realized by writing *Elixir Project*, I'd also create Elixir Project Experience and someday score a movie deal. These were both critical steps to achieving my ultimate why:

My Why: I must write Elixir Project so I can ignite one million souls by 2020.

Because 2020 came and went, you may wonder if I ever achieved my big why. (I'd want to know if I were you.) The good news is we did ignite one million souls and one year ahead of schedule. The movie deal is a different story for a different time. Just know I'm thrilled over a dozen producers are reading the script at this exact moment, some of which may make an offer.

In the space below, reflect on your Boon and then clarify your why. Be clear, concise, and direct.

My Why:

Claim Your Promise

Desire without a deadline is simply a pipe dream. It's easy to be fuzzy.

Writing down a date makes it real. Even if you miss the date, it creates accountability. You know if you've made it or missed it.

I committed to publishing *Elixir Project* in late 2015. It soon became obvious I was going to miss that date if I wanted to make the book everything I knew it needed to be. I eventually shifted the release date to December 6, 2016—my 40th birthday.

We launched the book in style. We set a world record for the largest ever livestream book release party with thousands tuning in from 180 events in 157 cities and six continents.

My promise: I will publish Elixir Project on December 6, 2016, with the world's largest livestream book release party.

In the space below, reflect on your Boon and claim your promise. Include a date too. Be clear, concise, and direct. It might feel scary, or silly, or both. But do it anyway.

I'm sure Edison, Ford, Oprah, and the Wright brothers felt scared and silly at times too. They did it anyway.

Remember, when you claim a promise, you demand something that's considered your due. It's not up for a vote, negotiation, or opinion. Results are irrelevant, and proof is unnecessary. You're simply telling the universe you're ready to assume possession of it. Claiming means you acknowledge the promise is already yours.

My Promise:

DAY 7

PROMOTION:

Inventory Your Promotion

I guess it comes down to a simple choice, really.
Get busy living or get busy dying.

—Andy Dufresne, *The Shawshank Redemption*

Are you too big to take on small assignments? What if those small assignments are in alignment with your ultimate idea? In my experience, Big Boons are often achieved through a series of small steps. This was the case for my sixth book—*Day Job to Dream Job*—when we launched it with Hollywood celebrities from *The Shawshank Redemption*.

This story sets up the second element: promotion.

FLAWLESS IDEA ANATOMY ELEMENT #2—PROMOTION

Small steps are often uneventful, unsexy, and underrated. This is why most people are unwilling to take them. They appear insignificant in the moment.

I didn't simply step on the stage in August 2014 with famous actors. Rather, one year before, I moved closer and closer to my 2013 Boon by taking on small assignments that were in alignment.

The initial idea to launch my sixth book at *The Shawshank Redemption* 20th Anniversary came into my awareness on June 18, 2013. I wish I could tell you I took immediate action. Unfortunately, I didn't.

I sat with the idea.

It floated around in my subconscious for over three-quarters of a year. Finally, on March 20, 2014, I took a small step by reaching out to a woman I had never met named Jodie.

I sent her the email below:

Subject: Author and 20 year Anniversary for Shawshank

I'd love to chat about the upcoming event in August. I am a speaker and author. My book, which releases on August 5, 2014, is all about Shawshank and escaping our Day Jobs. I wrote part of the book while sitting in the Reformatory last summer. The book is getting attention already nationally and internationally. I hired a *New York Times* bestselling illustrator who worked on all the images of the book (see one below). Many include elements of the Reformatory. It could be a nice promo for your event. I'd love to chat more.

From that email, we set up a phone call for the following day, March 21, 2014. Although I didn't know *what* to say or *how* to say it, I think Jodie caught my enthusiasm anyway. She followed up with an email later that day.

Hi, Kary!

I'm really excited about working with you and glad we could chat today!

A short promo video sounds great that I can show the Shawshank Committee on the 27th of this month. If you can email with some of the ideas we talked about (book signing at Renaissance Theatre on Friday evening; receive a book when a fan signs up for a Shawshank Package;

speaking event during the Anniversary, etc.) with your idea of cost for each, or complimentary, that would be really helpful for the committee.

Keep checking back on ShawshankTrail.com for the latest information. Or even visit us on our Facebook page!

Have a great weekend,
Jodie

Although I was out of town the following week for their meeting, I communicated my commitment through a written proposal. I've included this proposal below. You may want to read it, or you may want to skip it. Do whatever serves you and your Boon.

Over the years, many authors have asked me, "How did you get hundreds of thousands of dollars' worth of promotion for free?"

The temptation is to chalk it up to luck or chance. My personal favorite is when people say it *just* happened. Nothing ever *just* happens. There are a whole bunch of details packed into the word *just*.

If you read the proposal, you'll see how there's nothing *just* about it. Rather, I leveraged the second element that makes up all flawless ideas. Promotion!

Greetings Shawshank Committee,   March 26, 2014

I wish I could be hanging out with you this morning.

First, let me say I'm incredibly excited about the 20th Anniversary of *The Shawshank Redemption* on August 29, 30, and 31st. Similar to many other people, the movie was epic for me and represented hope in a very dark situation. I write about this journey in my forthcoming book, *Day*

Job to Dream Job, which releases in August 2014. I wrote part of the manuscript while sitting in a cell at the Ohio State Reformatory last June. I weave the *Shawshank* metaphor throughout my book. (You can read a little in the brief excerpt I sent to Jodie.)

I've spoken with Jodie at length about my heart to add value to you, your places of business, the local community, and the guests. I would love to partner with you for this special event. I don't want to overwhelm you with all kinds of ideas. (After all, we just met.) I'll list a few ideas below just to get things started.

My blog, website, books, and social media have a nice following, and my tribe would love to learn more about the Anniversary. I'd enjoy featuring links back to each of you too. The radio and TV interviews I typically receive during my book launches could create a cool synergistic partnership with your event.

I hope this letter captures my excitement, energy, and commitment to make the 20th Anniversary a transformational event. My desire is to serve and help you achieve your objectives for the event.

Obviously, my publisher loves it when I get the message of the book out to help people who are stuck. They also want the book to get as much media coverage as possible. I don't look to make a dime from the event or my role in the event. In fact, if we do this the right way, I believe my involvement could actually earn income back to your event and the historical society, etc.

Here are just some suggestions of what a partnership could look like:

- **Experiential Presentation**—I've given hundreds of presentations all over the country in every setting imaginable (colleges, universities, assemblies, corporate events, chapels, organizations, schools, retreats, etc.). My style is practical, interactive, experiential, relevant, and engaging. My presentation could include clips from *Shawshank* and how it relates to everyday life.

- **Complimentary Book with Ticket**—We could bundle a book with some or all Shawshank packages or museum prices, etc.

- **VIP session/Cocktail Reception**—I could be involved in the cocktail reception with celebrities. I could speak on how *The Shawshank Redemption* inspired me to write *Day Job to Dream Job*. Signed books could be provided with each ticket sold.

- **Signed Shawshank Illustrations**—I hired *New York Times* bestselling illustrator Mike Rohde to do illustrations in *Day Job to Dream Job*. Several of these are related to *The Shawshank Redemption* (see book excerpt for examples). These illustrations could be blown up, framed, and signed by Shawshank celebrities. Proceeds could go back to you (minus printing/production costs).

- **Gift Shops/Hotels**—*Day Job to Dream Job* could be sold at some or all locations. After the 20th Anniversary, the Ohio State Reformatory could sell the book, illustrations from *Day Job to Dream Job*, and/or a DVD I could produce especially for the gift shop related to people breaking free from the prison of their day jobs.

- **Book Signing**—This could be done at the Renaissance Theatre or another location. I believe a brief presentation about the book (with clear *Shawshank* integration) would help connect the dots for people. A book signing without a speaking presentation or program might be difficult. At the minimum, the book trailer could be shown if there was a book signing.

- **Book Trailer premiere shown before the movie at the Renaissance Theatre**—Next month, I am flying in a New York producer/actor to film a sixty-second book trailer that will be featured worldwide. The trailer will feature the Reformatory and show the symbolism between *Shawshank* and being imprisoned in your day job. I'll feature the trailer on my website: DayJobToDreamJob.com.

These ideas are just the beginning. I know more discussion will help bring additional clarity.

Blessings to you all.

Your friend and fellow Shawshank traveler,

Kary Oberbrunner

PROMOTION YIELDS POWER

Notice how I inventory my promotion throughout the email. This is an abnormal activity for most people. It might sound strange or even off-putting. Many times, we're so afraid we might position ourselves with arrogance that we swing to the other extreme—failing to position ourselves with any hint of confidence. In the name of false humility, we come off without any confidence, and we repel the Boon we're trying to attract.

Reread my letter again. Don't focus on *what* promotion I inventory; instead, focus on *how* I inventory. Most influencers want to partner with people who have experience. You want to demonstrate this isn't your first rodeo. After all, influencers are risking their reputation and platform on you.

Maybe you're tempted to think, *But I don't have much experience.* Remember, it's not the size of promotion—it's the scope. Size reflects *flashiness.* Scope reflects *faithfulness.* Influencers want to work with faithful people, those who do what they say and say what they do.

Look at this paragraph in particular:

Experiential Presentation—I've given hundreds of presentations all over the country in every setting imaginable (colleges, universities, assemblies, corporate events, chapels, organizations, schools, retreats, etc.) My style is practical, interactive, experiential, relevant, and engaging. My presentation could include clips from Shawshank and how it relates to everyday life.

Notice, I never describe the audiences where I spoke. Some events only had a few people in attendance. Other speeches I gave to a classroom of first-graders or a group of seniors at an assisted-living facility. I started speaking long ago at the age of eighteen when I preached to homeless men at the Milwaukee Rescue Mission. Most didn't listen. A few even fell asleep due to getting drunk earlier that day (or as a result of my monotone voice).

My letter wasn't arrogant. The truth is, I don't have much to brag about. I've had book signings where no one showed and conferences where we had to bring in extra plants and tables to make the room look fuller. Still, I didn't let those small beginnings hack me from my big Boon.

I've rarely been short on confidence. I use a strategy I learned from David, the shepherd boy who killed Goliath.

When selling and marketing himself to King Saul, he inventoried his promotion by referencing his previous victories over a lion and a bear.

Guess what? It worked! David's past successes convinced King Saul to promote him to a bigger future.

Facing the giant and then killing the giant was a result of saying yes to smaller assignments. These small assignments—killing the lion and bear—went largely unnoticed. (His sheep might have been the only ones that saw it.) Yet because David prepared for the moment, the moment was prepared for him.

Eventually, the world realized what David already knew—that he was ready for a bigger stage.

This principle isn't just contained in ancient stories. It's found in current ones too. Behind every successful person and every flawless idea, you'll discover this promotion principle. It was true for musicians like Justin Bieber, who started out on YouTube, athletes like former Green Bay Packer Jordy Nelson, who played college football as a walk-on, and Ellen Latham, who went from an unemployed single mother to co-founding Orangetheory Fitness, a multi-million dollar company.

Each dreamer stayed faithful to their idea. They inventoried their promotion long before they had a platform.

CLOSE YOUR GAP DAY 7: INVENTORY YOUR PROMOTION

For today's assignment, please inventory your promotion by answering these questions:

1. What smaller assignments have you completed that were in alignment with your ultimate Boon? (Please list them one-by-one.)

2. What did you learn by doing each of these smaller assignments?

3. How were these past assignments promotions to a bigger future?

4. Have you ever missed out on a promotion because, at the moment, you thought the assignment was too small? (If so, what new awareness will you take from this moving forward?)

5. What smaller assignment could you accept in the future that would put you in closer alignment with your ultimate Boon?

DAY 8

PROGRESS:
Track Your Progress

If there is no struggle, there is no progress.

—Frederick Douglass

I deas are like seeds.

Some ideas produce small things, and some produce big things. Some seeds yield fast results (like cornstalks), and some yield slow results (like redwoods).

Wisdom knows the difference between the two.

Consider the facts. Cornstalks barely survive one season, while giant redwoods can thrive for 1,200–1,800 years. Herein lies the problem. Most of us compare the speed of our redwood-sized idea with the speed of our neighbor's cornstalk-sized idea. When we do, we're tempted to stop putting in the effort. It seems easier to give up and quit. But quitting on your idea is the surest way to kill it.

Ideas almost always start beneath the surface. Like seeds, ideas are insignificant in the beginning. However, when planted in the right soil, the possibility of potential awakens the idea slowly and steadily.

This truth brings us to the third element: progress.

FLAWLESS IDEA ANATOMY ELEMENT #3—PROGRESS

I make it a point to celebrate progress, regardless of the size. The truth is most of the time, the progress of an idea is slow— so slow most people miss it or mock it.

It's understandable why we get discouraged. After all, we exert mountains of effort for very little impact—at least on the surface. But don't be fooled. Much is going on beneath the surface. During this testing time, our ideas dig deep roots.

This depth is essential because, without deep roots, our ideas can't support the weight of their impact once they break through the surface. *Deep roots mean rich fruit.*

The same thing was true with my Shawshank story. Yesterday, in Day 7, I told you about my idea to launch my book *Day Job to Dream Job* in 2014 at Shawshank prison with Hollywood celebrities. I began in 2013 by claiming my promise.

I knew launching the book on an international stage for the #1 movie of all time would help me move closer to my Big Why—igniting one million souls by 2020. Next, I wrote my Shawshank Proposal and sent it to Jodie. In it, I inventoried my promotion, demonstrating through past faithfulness how I was ready, willing, and able to play on a bigger stage.

Finally, I was now poised to sell and market my idea. I redefine selling as *serving* and marketing as *storytelling*. This is exactly what I did next. I showed up filled up and looked for ways to serve and tell stories.

I identified two clear actions:

1. *Serving: I bought them breakfast.*

I knew the Shawshank committee was going to meet on March 27, 2014. Because I couldn't make the meeting, I had breakfast delivered to them. Although it didn't cost me much financially, evidently, it made quite an impact. Jodie even took a picture and sent it to me.

I "sold" them through serving.

2. *Storytelling: I created a personal video for them.*

I asked for the names of everyone on the committee. Decked out in my Shawshank T-shirt, I shot a video on my smartphone and asked Jodie to play it at the breakfast. I shared the story of why Shawshank was special to me and how it was a metaphor for me going from my day job to my dream job. In the video, I mentioned each member by name and told him or her how excited I was to serve and make this event a smashing success for the public.

I "marketed" to them through storytelling.

CAN YOU SELL AND MARKET?

After coaching thousands of authors, speakers, and entrepreneurs, I've heard it all when it comes to fears about selling. Most people tell me they stink at sales and marketing. I listen, and I nod my head. And then I ask them two simple questions:

1. Can you serve?

2. Can you tell stories?

These same people stop and think, and then they chuckle. "Of course," they say with a smile. "Anyone can serve and tell stories."

Maybe anyone can, but hardly anyone does.

THE LETTER THAT DIDN'T LIE

Back to the Shawshank story. Remember, this is now only seven days after my very first email to Jodie. I didn't overthink it and hack myself. Rather, I took two simple action steps and positioned myself as an outlier in the process.

So, how was it received? Jodie told me in an email later that day:

Hi Kary,

THEY LOVED YOU!!!!!!!!

We opened the meeting with your video as they were nibbling on the delicious Panera goodies! I took a photo of the goodies with your picture on the table.

I told them all about the ideas you offered, and they all agreed that you should be a part of the Shawshank 20th Anniversary celebration.

The committee asked if there was a possibility of you joining us at our next meeting so they can meet you? It's Thursday, April 24, at 9:00 a.m. at the Reformatory. Because the meeting is early, the Quality Inn and Suites Mansfield would like to offer you a complimentary room on Wednesday, April 23!

I'm leaving for my next meeting and will be back in the office on Friday. Talk soon! Thank you again for making our meeting so special, Kary!

DON'T MISS THE MIRACLES

Some people might have missed the small seed that was growing. Others might have mocked it. How does writing a proposal, buying breakfast, and creating a video get me closer to my Boon? And what does any of that have to do with launching my book with Hollywood celebrities?

Me? I was elated because I knew the truth.

All these small steps had everything to do with achieving my Boon! I showed my wife the email and called my friend, David, and read him Jodie's response. Both of them probably thought I was a little crazy. I think they said, "That's nice."

Their response (or lack thereof) didn't sway me one bit. Deep inside, I knew I'd achieved a major victory. I knew that little seed was growing, and I celebrated the progress. Actually, I had been tracking my progress every step of the way:

1. When I located Jodie's name, *I celebrated.*

2. When I pressed send on my first email to Jodie, *I celebrated.*

3. When I wrote the first word of the proposal, *I celebrated.*

4. When I wrote the last word of the proposal, *I celebrated.*

5. When I ordered the Panera breakfast, *I celebrated.*

6. When I paid for the breakfast, *I celebrated.*

7. When I memorized each name for the video, *I celebrated.*

8. When I sent the video, *I celebrated.*

9. When I got Jodie's picture back, *I celebrated.*

10. When I got Jodie's email back, *I celebrated.*

I celebrated these ten things and probably one hundred more along the way. Whenever I'm pursuing my Boon, I often repeat a phrase:

Flawless doesn't mean fast. Flawless means forward.

As long as I'm taking action on my idea, then I'm moving forward. Even at times when I feel like I'm going backward, I redefine it as movement and celebrate.

You have a choice. Remember, you have a redwood-sized dream inside you. Results will probably not happen overnight. Because they often happen slowly over time, you need to track your progress. Failure to do so is hazardous to your mental health and lethal to your dream.

CLOSE YOUR GAP DAY 8: TRACK YOUR PROGRESS

For today's assignment, please track your progress by answering these questions:

1. Think back to your Boon. Big or small, have you seen any results yet? If so, list any and all evidence of progress:

2. Have you ever given up on a past Boon because you didn't see big enough results fast enough? After today's mission, what new commitments will you make going forward?

3. Is your Boon a cornstalk idea or a redwood idea? How do you know? Give evidence for your answer.

4. If you knew achieving your Boon was guaranteed if you didn't quit, would you keep putting in the effort? Why or why not?

5. What five actions can you take, big or small, to move closer to your Boon? Review the list and highlight the first action you will take. Now, choose to do that action within the next twenty-four hours.

DAY 9

POSTURE:

Strengthen Your Posture

Protect your enthusiasm from the negativity of others.

—H. Jackson Brown Jr.

A painted wood sign rests above the bookshelf in my office, serving as a constant reminder. Here's what it says:

If your dream doesn't scare you, dream bigger.

Every Boon should attract its share of critics and cynics. If it doesn't, it's probably too safe or too small. My hunch is that you have a big Boon, so naturally, you'll be on the receiving end of skepticism and criticism.

Although you can't control what others say about you or your Boon, you can control how you respond. Engaging with haters only hacks you. When you do, you lose focus by letting them inside your head and heart. You exchange *creating* for *combatting*.

If your goal is to prove you're right, you'll give your power away to others. But if your goal is to achieve your Boon, you can maintain your power by letting this fight strengthen your posture.

OPERATE WITH ENTHUSIASM

An enthusiastic posture is the answer. Enthusiasm literally means "possessed by God." When you're enthusiastic, you're aware of your relationship with the Divine. In times of discouragement, enthusiasm gives me all the confidence I need.

Rather than engaging in trivial squabbling with haters and critics, I acknowledge the truth—that my idea isn't my idea. It comes from above, and my responsibility is to implement my Boon.

With this in mind, the only true failure is a loss of enthusiasm. Winston Churchill understood this reality. He said, "Success consists of going from failure to failure without loss of enthusiasm."

His quote reveals the fourth and final element: posture.

FLAWLESS IDEA ANATOMY ELEMENT #4—POSTURE

Over the past few days, I've shared the first three elements of Flawless Idea Anatomy (promise, promotion, progress) within the context of my 2014 Boon: launching *Day Job to Dream Job* with Hollywood celebrities at *The Shawshank Redemption* 20th Anniversary.

We experienced minor setbacks all along the way. The movie agents didn't return phone calls. Certain guests didn't confirm. Yet throughout the process, I kept planning and preparing without loss of enthusiasm.

On that special weekend in August, I did become part of the lineup, and we did launch the book on an international stage. The event was featured in the *Daily Mail, The Hollywood Reporter, The New York Times,* the *Los Angeles Times,* and many other publications.

My experience isn't unique. When you study people who've achieved a big Boon, you'll see nearly everyone encountered circumstances that forced a gut check. In that moment, the choice was clear—*lie down or double down.*

We observe this moment of truth with Lindsey Stirling, the award-winning violinist who has scored billions of views on YouTube. Before the world knew her name, she performed on national television on *America's Got Talent.* She was far from award-winning, and the judges let her know. Seconds after her live performance, they delivered their opinions while friends, family, and millions of strangers listened. They said:

- You've got to be a world-class violinist ... or you'll miss loads of notes ... there were times when you sounded like a bunch of rats being strangled.

- You're not untalented, but you're not good enough to get away with flying through the air and trying to play the violin at the same time.

- You remind me of a little cartoon character. The problem with you is that you need to be in a group. You need a singer. I don't think what you are doing right now is enough to fill a theater in Vegas.[15]

It sounds sexy to say she was unmoved by their harsh critique. But Stirling now acknowledges the judges were right.

It took me years to realize that they weren't necessarily wrong. It's easy for people to look at it like, "Oh they messed up. They sure missed out on you." But looking at the video, I wasn't great. And it's not that they were wrong. And I think that's why it hurt so bad when I was on the show and I got kicked off and when they said really mean things to me. It hurt so bad because it was kind of true, and I think the truth hurts way more. And they were right. I hadn't earned or developed the skills to be able to dance, to be thrown around up in the air while playing the violin. It's really difficult.[16]

Thankfully, she didn't settle for their story. Rather, she chose to write a new one (see Day 1—Write Your Story). She proved the critics wrong by strengthening her posture.

The key is to remain enthusiastic even when the results don't give you any reason to rejoice. You can see this modeled by an incredibly popular musical group from my own backyard.

Humble Beginnings

Although they literally fill stadiums now, in 2011, Twenty One Pilots traveled to their first show outside their city. Guess how many people came to an unimpressive basement to hear them perform.

Twelve people!

If you watch the clip from that show, you'll realize Tyler Joseph and Josh Dun didn't hold back.[17] And after making it big, they embodied enthusiasm playing in front of twelve thousand people as in front of the first twelve. Years later at the Grammys—the television season's most-watched entertainment telecast—in front of more than twenty million viewers on February 12, 2017, they accepted the Award for the Best Pop Duo/Group Performance with the same enthusiasm.

Here's the secret:

Enthusiasm isn't a result of being on a bigger stage.
Enthusiasm is what gets you on a bigger stage.
Enthusiasm is the cause, not the effect.
It's the root, not the result.

If you can't get excited in front of twelve people, then twelve thousand or twelve million aren't going to do it for you either.

I've been writing books for over sixteen years, and I've been doing events longer than that. I'll never forget one of the first events I did. Seven people showed up. This was before I had a team or even someone to help me pass out the name tags.

Was I discouraged that less than 10% of my goal came?

Not at all! I treated those seven people like kings and queens.

I once had a book signing where no one showed—um make that two book signings without a single visitor. The key is, I kept going. Fast-forward to today. We've done hundreds of live events and even more online ones. We've had tens of thousands of people attend, but I'm as enthused today as I was back at my first event with those seven people.

Although we've encountered our share of setbacks, we strengthened our posture and maintained enthusiasm throughout.

CLOSE YOUR GAP DAY 9: STRENGTHEN YOUR POSTURE

For today's assignment, answer these questions:

1. What if no one supports you or your Boon? How will you feel? And more importantly, how will you respond?

2. What are three practical ways you can strengthen your posture and increase your enthusiasm right now?

3. How would you approach your Boon differently if you truly understood your Boon has been entrusted to you from above?

4. From this day forward, with your Boon in mind, will you make a conscious commitment to

- Turn your setbacks into comebacks?

  YES ☐   NO ☐

- Let this fight become the fuel to strengthen your posture?

  YES ☐   NO ☐

- Operate with enthusiasm?

  YES ☐   NO ☐

DAY 10

CREATION:
Create Your Idea

Everything is created twice, first in the mind and then in reality.

—Robin Sharma, *The Monk Who Sold His Ferrari*

H ave you said any of these statements since starting this book?

I don't know my Boon yet.
My idea still feels fuzzy.
How can I be sure I'm headed in the right direction?

If you have had any of these thoughts, you're normal. None of us wants to get it wrong, look dumb, or feel foolish.

Ironically, though, staying with any of these statements has never produced anything positive. Here's the truth from my experience:

I never know anything for sure.
My ideas always feel fuzzy in the beginning.
I'm rarely 100% clear about my Boons.

Despite my uncertainty, I know one thing for sure: The right step is always the one requiring action. Most people don't like that answer. They want clarity *before* they take action. But clarity only comes *because* we take action.

The way forward is never smooth, clear, or obvious in the beginning. Ask any innovator. Most of us tell God, the universe, our friends and family, or anyone who will listen, "Once I know *all* the steps, then I'll take the *first* step."

We want a map of all 229 steps so we can see exactly where the path leads. But this mindset is completely contrary to the way Unhackability works. Step 229—just like step two—is often hidden from us, and it should be.

We don't deserve to know step two if we're unwilling to take step one. Besides, if we knew step two ahead of time, we'd be overwhelmed and stop before starting. Here's another truth most people miss: Once you take a few steps, you change into a very different person. This is intentional. Each step grows you into a bigger person who can handle a bigger step.

The more steps you take, the more *committed* you feel, and the more *capable* you become. Besides, you're not supposed to know how it finishes. You're only supposed to know how it starts. We see this beautifully in the life of Kyle Maynard.

A CONCEPT CALLED FIRST CREATION

Kyle had a big Boon—to climb Mount Kilimanjaro. That's tough for anybody. But he had a little problem: Kyle was born without any hands or feet. He's a congenital amputee.

His Boon to climb Mount Kilimanjaro included the four elements essential for Flawless Idea Anatomy.

1. He claimed his *promise.*

When he spoke to ABC News in 2011—a few months before his climb attempt—Kyle explained his vision:

A main mission behind the climb will be to "send a message" to veterans who have been disabled and to disabled children around the world "to show that there are challenges in life, but it doesn't mean that you have to give up. You decide how you're going to draw meaning from the challenges in your life."[18]

2. He inventoried his *promotion.*

Kyle didn't start with the idea to climb a 20,000-foot-tall mountain. This big Boon was the result of a long series of smaller Boons he'd achieved. Each of these smaller Boons helped him grow into a bigger person with a bigger Boon. Notice his path of promotion:

- At age eleven, Kyle played nose tackle for the Collins Hill National Eagles football team.

- He wrestled in high school, ultimately winning thirty-six matches in his senior year of high school.

- He was awarded the title of GNC's World's Strongest Teen by bench pressing twenty-three repetitions of 240 lbs.

- He received the ESPN Espy Award for Best Athlete With A Disability in 2004.

- He appeared in both *Vanity Fair* and the Abercrombie & Fitch *Stars on the Rise* catalog.

- He was the recipient of the 2004 President's Award for the Sports Humanitarian Hall of Fame.

- He went on to attend the University of Georgia and was a part of their wrestling team but left shortly after starting his education to promote his book and pursue a speaking career.

- While attending the University of Georgia, he began work as a speaker for the Washington Speaker's Bureau, specializing in motivational speeches.

- He was featured on talk shows, including *The Oprah Winfrey Show* and *Larry King Live*.

- He wrote the *New York Times* bestselling autobiography *No Excuses: The True Story of a Congenital Amputee Who Became a Champion in Wrestling and in Life*.

- He was inducted into both the Georgia State Wrestling Hall of Fame and the National Wrestling Hall of Fame in Oklahoma.

- In 2007, he competed in his first MMA fight.

- In 2008, Maynard opened No Excuses CrossFit gym, a CrossFit intensive facility located in Suwanee, Georgia.

3. He tracked his *progress.*

In the beginning, Kyle didn't know how he'd achieve his Boon. Nobody ever does. But he didn't let that stop him. Rather than focusing on perfection, he focused on action. He took the first step—literally. And then he tracked his progress.

It began in Colorado with a few hotel towels and a roll of duct tape. An article for the Gwinnet Daily Post describes his training.[19] Soon after Maynard was introduced to Dan Adams, who became a co-leader of the excursion dubbed Mission Kilimanjaro, the duo found themselves out West and trying to figure out a way for Maynard to go hiking. The only way for Maynard to do it was to essentially bear crawl, leaving the ends of his nubs vulnerable. Thus they used the towels and duct tape to fashion some admittedly ill-conceived protective gear.

"It's definitely not a succeeded-out-of-the-first-gate type of thing," Maynard said with a laugh. Over time and several trial runs, they tried a number of different things—oven mitts, kayaking foam placed inside chalk bags placed inside pieces of mountain bike tires, and eventually specially molded carbon fiber gloves and boots. "Really the training process has been refining our equipment, finding what works and doesn't work," Adams said. "Each time we've gotten a little more efficient."

4. He strengthened his *posture.*

Remember, Kyle climbed by staring straight at the ground, bear crawling for days and days on end. There was nothing easy about his posture—physically speaking. However, all along the way to his Boon, Kyle chose to strengthen his posture—mentally speaking.

> 95% of it does suck. I'm staring at the dirt. I'm not even able to go and talk to my friends and see the beautiful views unless I stop and sit down and look. But that 5% that doesn't suck … it's amazing. Getting to a place that there's no way my wheelchair could have brought me—that's what I love. I want to go out there and have my life mean something. When I've gotten down and I've seen the mountain, and I see what we've achieved, it's like WOW! Maybe that was a really bad idea that we were there, but it was beautiful.[20]

CLOSE YOUR GAP DAY 10: CREATE YOUR IDEA

For today's assignment, please create your idea by completing something we call a Boon Sheet. Unhackable people realize every Boon includes a

WHO
WHAT
WHEN
WHERE
WHY
HOW

This is the framework I use to create everything in my life and business. It's how I partnered with Hollywood celebrities to launch my book. It's how the six modules in Author Academy Elite are organized. And it's how I structure every live event and online masterclass.

Focus on your idea by doing your own Boon Sheet. Before you begin, reflect upon three important words Kyle Maynard said:

I don't know.

Here's the full context of his comment:

I said I want to climb Mount Kilimanjaro. I was like how the heck are we going to? Three words: *I don't know.* Those three words are three of the most important words of my life. All discoveries happen from I don't know. I don't know if I can. I don't know if I can't. But I do know that I want to try and figure it out. I want to go and find a way to get up there.[21]

And now, it's time to complete your own Boon Sheet. Don't overthink it. And please don't aim for perfection. Action is the goal. You won't have clarity at this point. You might not even know your Boon. Fill it out as best as you know at this moment in time.

You're not on trial, and there is no judge—especially your internal one. Consider Kyle if you're tempted to go into freak-out mode. He bear-crawled up a mountain with bath towels duct-taped to his four nubs.

Kind of puts things in perspective, doesn't it?

This is sacred work you're doing, something we call first creation. Choose to be a victor and take imperfect action. If you still feel panicky or fuzzy, simply preface each of your answers with "my best guess at this moment in time is ..."

Now, go complete your Boon Sheet and remember to have fun.

BOON SHEET

Who: *Who does my Boon involve?*

What: *What is my Boon?*

When: *When will my Boon be experienced?*

Where: *Where will my Boon be experienced?*

Why: *Why must I do this Boon?*

How: *How will I do my Boon (the very first action only)?*

DAY 11

TIME:
Write Your Check

Einstein was right, you can be in two places at once.

—Steve Connor, Science Editor, *Independent*

The biggest threat to your Boon isn't skeptics or cynics. It's you and, more specifically, your unbelief. We don't need to worry about doubters or haters out there. We need to worry about the doubters and haters in here—inside each one of us.

In the context of your Boon, two of the most common objections you'll encounter are time and space. Maybe you've even said them yourself:

My Boon hasn't happened yet. (Time Objection)
I can't see my Boon yet. (Space Objection)

Today, we'll address the time objection and tomorrow the space objection.

A CONCEPT CALLED SECOND CREATION

To better understand first creation and second creation, read this excerpt from *Elixir Project*:

> *"Okay, five minutes left. Let me give the quantum physics piece a try," Damon says. "In class, we've been studying the famous double-slit experiment and how matter can be in two places at one time. So why wouldn't this be true with ideas, too? Ideas are thoughts, and thoughts are electrical energy. This means they have electrons, and we know electrons can exist in two places at once."*

> *"So ideas exist in two places at once, too," Damon and I both say in unison.*

> *"That was freaky," Karme jokes.*

> *I see where Damon is going now and jump in to get us there faster. "Ideas manifest in the mind of the person imagining the thought," I say. "And that same idea exists somewhere else in the universe simultaneously."*

> *Phoenix smiles and adds to the energy of the conversation. "Just like this athletic center. The architect imagined it. When he did, he created it in his mind the first time. Years later, when the final brick was laid, he created the idea a second time. Ideation and implementation. First creation and second creation."*

> *"Does that mean if you think it, you can do it?" Karme asks.*

> *"Even crazier," Damon says. "It means if you think it, you've already done it."*

TWO PLACES AT ONCE

Although it's not necessary to understand the finer points of quantum mechanics to become Unhackable, it's important you're aware of quantum entanglement, namely that matter can exist in two places at once. Whether you agree with the science or not is irrelevant. It's true nonetheless.

Notice the following progression that I refer to as Unhackability Entanglement©.

Matter can exist in two places at once.

Ideas are thoughts, and thoughts are electrical energy.

Ideas have electrons, and electrons can exist
in two places at once.

Ideas can exist in two places at once.

An idea manifests in the mind of the person
imagining the thought.
(First Creation)

That same idea exists somewhere else
in the universe simultaneously.
(Second Creation)

SCIENCE AND FAITH AGREE

Perhaps you wonder how faith and science can coexist, at least on the topic of Unhackability Entanglement. By reviewing ancient literature, it's clear that Scripture acknowledges the existence of both first creation and second creation.

Everyone who looks at a woman with lust for her has already committed adultery with her in his heart.
—Matthew 5:28 (NASB)

According to Jesus, in the record books of heaven, if we imagine an idea with our mind (first creation) we've also created the action in our heart (second creation). It gets even crazier. We'll be judged and rewarded based upon those ideas we imagine.

Jesus gave other instances, positive and negative, where there is no separation between time or space and our ideas.

Truly I tell you, whatever you bind on earth will be bound in heaven, and whatever you loose on earth will be loosed in heaven.
—Matthew 18:18

Similar to quantum mechanics with atoms, according to Jesus, there is no division between what happens in heaven and earth. Albert Einstein referred to this entanglement concept as "spooky action from a distance."

We'll get to our daily mission in a moment, but rest assured, faith and science are full of examples where someone thought or did something over here and it affected someone or something immediately over there. We observe this with the healing of the centurion's servant:

When Jesus had entered Capernaum, a centurion came to him, asking for help. "Lord," he said, "my servant lies

85

at home paralyzed, suffering terribly." Jesus said to him, "Shall I come and heal him?"

The centurion replied, "Lord, I do not deserve to have you come under my roof. But just say the word, and my servant will be healed. For I myself am a man under authority, with soldiers under me. I tell this one, 'Go,' and he goes; and that one, 'Come,' and he comes. I say to my servant, 'Do this,' and he does it."

When Jesus heard this, he was amazed. ... Then Jesus said to the centurion, "Go! Let it be done just as you believed it would." And his servant was healed at that moment.

Talk about experiencing the very definition of abracadabra: *it came to pass as it was spoken.* Jesus had the idea, and in the same moment, the idea was implemented. There was no gap between dreaming and doing. Those who observed this called it a miracle—and it was. However, is there a scientific explanation too?

THE MIRACLE FOUND IN SCIENCE

Science has confirmed this phenomenon though cutting-edge experiments. In *Nature*—the international weekly journal of science—we read the following:

Objects can be in multiple states simultaneously: for example, an atom can be in two places, or spin in opposite directions, at once. Measuring an object forces it to snap into a well-defined state. Furthermore, the properties of different objects can become "entangled," meaning that their states are linked: when a property of one such object is measured, the properties of all its entangled twins become set, too.[22]

Speaking of twins, human twins often experience a unique phenomenon.

> It's a popular myth that identical twins ... can sometimes sense when one of the pair is in danger, even if they're oceans apart. Scientists cast a skeptical eye over such claims, largely because it isn't clear how these weird connections could possibly work. Yet they've had to come to terms with something that's no less strange in the world of physics: an instantaneous link between particles that remains strong, secure, and undiluted no matter how far apart the particles may be—even if they're on opposite sides of the universe. It's a link that Einstein went to his grave denying, yet its existence is now beyond dispute. Its name is entanglement.[23]

Readers who don't agree with science or Scripture may be tempted to chalk up this entire section to wishful thinking. Maybe they don't understand it, or maybe they don't *want* to understand it. But it's similar to other universal laws—like gravity. You don't have to agree with gravity or understand it, but you're governed by it nonetheless. (If you step off a building, you'll get reminded on the way down.)

It's to our advantage to respect universal laws. When we leverage the law of gravity, we can create powerful outcomes like air travel or cities full of skyscrapers. When we deny the law of gravity, we can end up dead or seriously injured.

THE $10 MILLION CHECK

Maybe you know the story of the $10 million check? It even found its way onto Oprah's show in 1997 when Jim Carrey shared it. This comedic actor grew up in a family so poor that, for a time, they lived in their Volkswagen van on a relative's lawn. Though many people pegged Carrey as following the family pattern of poverty, he believed differently.

Carrey knew he had a greater calling on his life. At the age of ten years old, he even mailed his resume to *The Carol Burnett Show*. He never lost hope or the idea of becoming wealthy. It was his Boon, and no one could take it from him.

One night in 1992, when he was a struggling young comic trying to make his way in Los Angeles, he drove his old beat-up Toyota to the top of a hill. While sitting there looking down over the city and dreaming of his future, he wrote himself a check for $10 million dollars. He put in the memo line "for acting services rendered" and dated it for Thanksgiving 1995. He stuck that check in his wallet—and carried it with him for years.

Right before Thanksgiving three years later, he discovered he would receive $10 million dollars for his role in *Dumb & Dumber*.[24]

Carrey leveraged the universal law mentioned above. He created the mental image and took action by writing the check. Three years passed before he possessed that sum of money. Instead of letting time hack him, he transcended it.

Carrey's Boon Check included three important components—dollars, date, and description. Notice what he wrote:

Dollars: $10 Million
Date: Thanksgiving 1995
Description: For acting services rendered

CLOSE YOUR GAP DAY 11: WRITE YOUR CHECK

This process of first creation and second creation plays a significant role in Flawless Idea Anatomy, becoming Unhackable, and achieving your Boon.

Ready or not, I'm inviting you to write your Boon Check. I've made it easy by including one here. You can scan it, print it, and carry it in your wallet or post it on your bathroom mirror. For those people digitally inclined, you can snap a photo of it with your phone and use it as your wallpaper or background.

Please include the three important components on your Boon Check: dollars, date, and description.

Boon Check

		1206
UNHACKABILITY	DATE _____	
BOON CHECK		
PAY TO THE ORDER OF _____	$ [ ]	
_____	DOLLARS 🔒	
FOR _____	_____	

⑈⅃00000000⑈ ⑈000⑃ 2030⑈

Dollars

Money always brings up a slew of feelings. In our private thoughts, we often wonder if we should have money or if we're worth money. Many people get hacked just thinking about money.

Money is simply a *tool* and can be used for good or bad. It isn't evil, and it gives us options. Money doesn't ruin us—it simply reveals us. It's like a magnifying glass, and it brings us to the surface in a bigger, bolder way.

If you're still nervous about writing an amount for yourself, then write it for someone else. Give that sum away to a charity of your choice. Maybe you're getting hacked another way—thinking your Boon isn't worth anything at all. Or you wonder if anyone will pay you for your Boon. This type of thinking is unproductive.

Nothing would have ever been created if the inventors doubted the value before they started. Paperclips, plastic bags, straws, and sticky notes probably seemed like pretty stupid ideas in the beginning too. But today, they've earned millions and millions of dollars.

Date

Take your best shot and quit aiming for perfection. Instead, take imperfect action. Pick a date. Put your idea on paper and make it real.

Description

If Jim Carrey—Mr. Funny Guy himself—had enough clarity to choose a description, then you can too. He wrote *For acting services rendered*. Write your Boon on the line and reduce it to one sentence.

For my Boon, I wrote *For Elixir Project Film.*

If you feel stretched or uncomfortable by this activity—good! You're growing, and growth is essential to becoming Unhackable.

DAY 12

SPACE:

See Your Space

If you can dream it, you can do it.

—Walt Disney

Yesterday, we explored the time objection: *My Boon hasn't happened yet.* Today, we'll explore the space objection: *I can't see my Boon yet.* To do so, you'll meet a cartoonist, a rabbi, an author, and an innovator. Each person will reveal a truth about how the space objection exists only within our minds.

THE CARTOONIST

Mike Vance, former dean of Disney University, tells this story of Walt Disney's legacy in his book *Think Out of the Box*:

> A journalist, knowing Walt was seriously ill, persisted in getting an interview with Walt and was frustrated on numerous occasions by the hospital staff. When he finally

managed to get into the room, Walt couldn't sit up in bed or talk above a whisper.

Walt instructed the reporter to lie down on the bed next to him, so he could whisper in the reporter's ear. For the next thirty minutes, Walt and the journalist lay side by side as Walt referred to an imaginary map of Walt Disney World on the ceiling above the bed. Walt pointed out where he planned to place various attractions and buildings. He talked about transportation, hotels, restaurants, and many other parts of his vision for a property that wouldn't open to the public for another six years.[25]

Walt died on December 15, 1966.

The Magic Kingdom opened on October 1, 1971.

Soon after the completion of The Magic Kingdom at Walt Disney World, someone said, "Isn't it too bad Walt Disney didn't live to see this?" Vance replied, "He did see it. That's why it's here."

Truth #1: A clear Boon can outlive you.

THE RABBI

You might remember Jesus' darkest day. He was in the garden of Gethsemane about to be betrayed by Judas, one of his own disciples. Despite his pleas for support from his three closest friends, they fell asleep, and he was left all alone to contemplate his impending trial and death by crucifixion. Jesus was in so much pain and mental anguish that "his sweat was like drops of blood falling to the ground."[26]

He had nowhere else to turn and nothing else to do except pour out his heart to his Father. You'd think he would have reflected on his present pain. But instead, he focused on his future Boon.

Weird? Of course. But weirder yet is one particular phrase. Notice the Greek phrase and subsequent English translation:

Greek: ὅπου ἐγὼ εἰμὶ

English: "Father, I want those you have given me to be with me *where I am*, and to see my glory, the glory you have given me because you loved me before the creation of the world."[27]

Jesus prayed for his future followers and said he wanted them to be where he is. Did he mean in the Upper Room at the Last Supper or in the Garden of Gethsemane? He leveraged a different strategy by remembering his future. (Think back to Day 5: Count Your Cost.)

Similar to how Walt Disney lay in his hospital bed and saw the Magic Kingdom, Jesus lay on cushions at the Last Supper and saw the heavenly Kingdom. He was moments away from incredible pain, but that wasn't his focus. Instead, Jesus visited a future space and wished his future followers could be with him where he *is*—present tense.

Talk about overcoming the space objection. By seeing his future Boon, he transcended his present pain.

Truth #2: You can see your future Boon within your present pain.

THE AUTHOR

As you've hopefully come to realize by now, Unhackability isn't theory. It's not about only experts or outliers. It's about people like you and me.

For this reason, I'll be the next example and reference part of my story because maybe you can relate. I wasn't born into privilege or position. In first grade, I was a kid diagnosed with a learning disability because of a severe stuttering problem.

Like any young adult, I experienced pain and loss. But because my words betrayed me, I kept my feelings inside. Without the ability to communicate, I expressed my emotion and angst with self-injury.

Over time, it turned into cutting. Through my college years, I kept this secret to myself by pretending. In truth, I was conflicted, believing a lie, and at times, I felt like escaping through suicide.

I followed this dark path until grace woke me up in the form of my wife, Kelly. Slowly, the layers of shame and performance fell away until I emerged into freedom.

All throughout those difficult years, I had a dream of writing. As the vision for my Boon grew, so did my visibility. This is how Unhackability works.

When I was four years old, my grandmother bought me a book with my name in the front. It planted an idea about me writing my own book someday.

At five years old, I wrote my first story about Mighty, the robot, and Michael, his owner. I kept writing through the years—poetry, stories, and articles.

My junior year in college, I sent a bunch of my writing to a real published author. I asked him for his professional opinion. His gracious letter encouraged me and helped me see my future space—life as a full-time writer.

As the years passed, I encountered my share of rejection letters. Sometimes, I felt like giving up on my Boon. Other times, I wondered if I had the wrong Boon.

Still, I kept moving toward it, regardless of what others said. And after years of trying, in 2003, I finally got a publishing contract for my first book: *The Journey Toward Relevance.* I saw myself as an author, even when the rejection letters told me otherwise. The longer I kept my vision in front of me, the more my visibility grew. Like Walt and Jesus, with persistence and patience, I eventually overcame the space objection too.

Truth #3: Vision grows visibility.

THE INNOVATOR

Steve Jobs, one of the most innovative people of this century, perfected the art of seeing his space long before colleagues or contemporaries did. In this process, he didn't waste time trying to connect the dots looking forward. Rather, he realized a brilliant truth:

> You can't connect the dots looking forward; you can only connect them looking backward. So you have to trust that the dots will somehow connect in your future. You have to trust in something—your gut, destiny, life, karma, whatever. Because believing that the dots will connect down the road will give you the confidence to follow your heart, even when it leads you off the well-worn path.[28]

Truth #4: You can only connect the dots looking backward.

CLOSE YOUR GAP DAY 12: SEE YOUR SPACE

Ask those who know me best, and they'll agree—if you give me a whiteboard and a dry erase marker, I'm suddenly armed and dangerous. I certainly can't draw, but that's not the point. For some reason, when I'm holding a dry erase marker, I'm able to see my space much clearer.

My phone is full of pictures of whiteboards from past sessions. These whiteboards are covered with words and pictures. In meetings, my teammates often sit while I stand. I talk out what I see, and I write thoughts and ideas on the board. They push back, ask questions, or listen.

Entire books and businesses were outlined on whiteboards as I saw my space unfold right before my eyes. I always took a picture of it and archived it so I wouldn't forget.

Now it's your turn. Today, I'd like you to see your space. You can write out your thoughts on the whiteboard below, or you can grab a physical piece of paper and draw it out. You might even have access to a real whiteboard, or maybe you prefer creating a vision board instead.

The point is this—start seeing your space. When you do, you'll overcome the space objection.

I'm purposely not listing rules or strict guidelines for today's mission. Walt, Jesus, Steve, and I all did this space thing differently. It's not *how* we did it that matters. Rather, it's *that* we did it.

No matter what your strategy is, just keep your writing utensil moving. Put words or pictures on a page. When you're done, snap a picture with your phone and archive it. You'll never again be able to say, "I can't see my Boon yet."

The Space I See Looks Like This

PART 3

DAY 13

URGENCY:
Establish Your Deadline

The ultimate inspiration is the deadline.

—Nolan Bushnell

elcome to the second component in the Unhackable Circle©. Over the past few days, we've explored the first component—Idea (Flawless Idea Anatomy). Now, it's time to take a deep dive into the second one—Focus (Deliberate Magnetic Focus).

Before we get to the *fun* part, it would be wise to explore the *facts* part. If you don't want the facts, then jump down to the fun part because it truly is fun. You'll take a mental vacation to a beautiful oceanside thinking space. (Seriously.)

However, if you skip the facts, you won't fully understand what today's high performers like you are up against. On that note, I invite you to press pause on the ocean for a few more minutes. Dive into the facts first and then experience all the sandy shores you want.

Deal?

THE FACTS!

So, how bad is it?

According to research by several futurists and Buckminster Fuller's Knowledge Doubling Curve, humanity finds itself on the precipice of yet another new world order.[29] Here's why.

Imagine all the knowledge gained from the beginning of time to the year AD 1. If that knowledge represents one unit, then it took 1,500 years—until the sixteenth century—for this information to double from one to two units.[30]

Because this progress was so gradual, humanity adapted to these advancements and the shift from the first order to the second order quite well. As history moved on, we built upon the facts and findings of our predecessors. This resulted in the next doubling of knowledge—from two to four units—taking less than 250 years. Even then, society adapted well because our life spans were shorter. Innovation and change came, but at a bearable pace.

The next leap forward took even less time—picture a train traveling down a mountain, picking up momentum. In this third order, the next doubling of knowledge—from four to eight units—took less than twenty-five years.[31] Family systems began showing signs of strain. Grandparents, parents, and kids each felt they had grown up in a unique world with unique circumstances and rules.

As time marched on, knowledge increased exponentially—doubling every year and then every month. In 2010, Eric Schmidt, the former CEO of Google, made a profound statement: All the information ever created in human history up to 2003 is now created every two days.[32] IBM predicted back in 2013 that knowledge would double every twelve hours in 2020.[33] Today's experts adjusted that number to every second, and maybe even faster.

This rate of change was already too fast for most. Some believe our society has become increasingly volatile—that humans can no longer endure the physical, emotional, and mental stress of such rapid adaptation. Refer to the images below to see this type of exponential change.

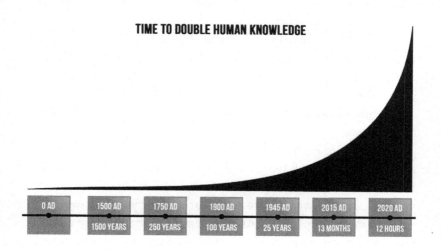

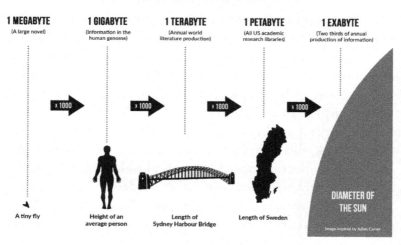

Today, every person in the civilized world experiences a *daily* rate of change that was formerly spread out over 1,500 *years*. We gloss over facts like this because it's difficult to comprehend, but let me give you another example to help the metaphor connect.

Imagine waking up one day at 9:00 a.m. without any past knowledge of travel. You begin by traveling on foot. Then, you quickly shift to traveling via canoe and then horse, chariot, ship, stagecoach, railroad, automobile, airplane, and finally, spaceship. Consider the mental energy required to make those adaptations.

Now, imagine that change isn't taking place over thousands of years where you have time to process. Instead, those changes take place within a two-hour period. Although mind-boggling, you'd still have twenty-two hours of change yet to experience. And in my metaphor, I only referenced one day. The truth is you'd experience an entire lifetime of days strung together at this rate of change.

DISTRACTIONS CALLED DOPAMINE LOOPS

This sheer amount of information is overwhelming for anyone. Overwhelm isn't a good thing, because the more we feel it, the more dopamine distractions we crave. Getting a dopamine fix serves as a coping mechanism that helps us process increasing levels of stress. If we're not careful, this creates the perfect conditions for an addiction.

According to her article in *Psychology Today*, Susan Weinschenk, PhD, explains why dopamine delivered though our smartphones fosters such a powerful addiction. "Dopamine starts you seeking, then you get rewarded for the seeking, which makes you seek more. It becomes harder and harder to stop looking at email, stop texting, or stop checking your cell phone to see if you have a message or a new text."[34]

Most people aren't even aware they are addicted until they try to separate from their smartphones.[35] Such a withdrawal can result in symptoms such as depression, insomnia, and anxiety.

With this in mind, it's easy to see why much of the population gets hacked on a daily basis. The odds are certainly against us. Simply put, the exponential growth of information and technology seriously threatens our ability to focus.

Decades ago there were only three channels on television. Focusing wasn't as difficult. However, when we have billions of options interrupting us every day—and at our fingertips, predominantly through our smartphones—maintaining Deliberate Magnetic Focus is nearly impossible.

SMARTPHONES INTERRUPTING SEX

If you've ever checked your phone for no reason, you're not alone. Many people recheck it despite having checked it a few seconds ago. Without even consciously thinking, we turn the screen on to make sure we haven't missed out on any notification, call, or message.

On topic, most phone addicts experience phantom vibrations. This behavior is described as a belief your phone is ringing or has received a notification even though it has not. About 90% of people have felt false vibrations, and around 30% have heard ringing that simply did not exist.[36]

Phantom vibrations aren't the only recent behavior modification. Check out these other smartphone statistics:

- According to a Nielsen report, the average teenager sent and received 3,339 texts per month.[37]

- 46% of Americans admitted to checking their smartphones before they even get out of bed in the morning.[38]

- 75% of people keep their phones on all day and night, not turning them off to go to bed.[39]

- One in three people confesses to checking their email in the middle of the night. 50% of people ages eighteen to twenty-four do this.[40]

- 69% of people can't go to bed without checking their inbox.[41]

- 40% of the population is addicted to their smartphones, according to an article in *Psychology Today*.[42]

- 58% of men and 47% of women suffer from nomophobia, i.e., the fear of being without a smartphone.[43]

- 84% of people say they couldn't even give up their smartphone for a single day.[44]

- 88% of Americans admit to using their smartphones while in the bathroom. (The other 12% might be lying.)[45]

- 9% of people have used their mobile device during sex, from checking text messages to answering phone calls.[46] The number of people checking smartphones while having sex rises to 20% among the ages of eighteen to thirty-four.[47]

- Nearly one in three Americans would rather give up all forms of sex for three months than trade in their smartphone for a "dumbphone" for one week.[48]

- The *Mobile Consumer Habits* study reports 12% of people use their phones while they are in the shower.[49]

- Nearly three in four American smartphone users surveyed said they are within five feet of their devices the majority of the time.[50]

- 7% of individuals state that excessive cell phone use caused them to lose a relationship or job.[51]

A NEW CONDITION CALLED DIGIPHRENIA

Up until the last century, the possibility of being two places at once was debatable. However, in our current century, the debate is now over. Look no further than the word *digiphrenia* and you'll discover why.

The root words *digi* and *phrenia* mean digital and disordered condition of mental activity. At its core, digiphrenia represents an abnormal state of mental activity that results from the constant bombardment of digital input.

The term was popularized by author Douglas Rushkoff in his book *Present Shock*. According to him, we created a world where we try to exist in more than one sphere, simultaneously and in parallel. In his interview with NPR, he defined digiphrenia as "existing in more than one incarnation of yourself at the same time."[52]

Rather than being single-minded and present, our focus is distracted and fragmented. We have multiple personalities to maintain—our *online* life and our *real* life. The concept is exacerbated even further when we consider multiple online platforms. Our identity on Twitter must reconcile with our profile on Instagram, Facebook, and LinkedIn, for example. Throw in a few more social media accounts and professional platforms, and suddenly, our multiple personalities require more effort and energy than any single human can manage.

The urban dictionary defines digiphrenia as "the constant insane dual personalities people are immersed in between their phones and the real life around them."[53] Robert E. Fisher, MD, goes on to explain, "In this digitally provoked mental condition, we live with myriad distractions that take our focus away from the immediacy of who we are with, and the purpose of that encounter."[54]

You can probably relate to this experience—dinnertime with friends who are there but not *really* there. Rather than being absorbed in the conversation, they're absorbed with their smartphones instead. It's not just our friends who are guilty. It's us too.

A 2018 article in *Time* magazine boldly begins, "Whether you know it or not, you've been phubbed. ... 'Phubbing'—snubbing someone you're talking to to look at a cell phone—may not be part of your everyday vocabulary, but it's almost certainly part of your everyday life."[55]

Ouch!

The word emerged in 2012. It was a term coined as part of a campaign by Macquarie Dictionary to describe the habit of snubbing someone in favor of a mobile phone.[56] "Phubbing was found to threaten four 'fundamental needs'—belongingness, self-esteem, meaningful existence and control—by making phubbed people feel excluded and ostracized."[57]

As you might expect, phubbing and digiphrenia pose a threat to your Boon as well as your health. Digiphrenia has actually killed many people in many ways. Phone users have walked off cliffs to their death, unaware of the dangers because they focused too much on their screen.[58] Even more of an epidemic today is how prevalent texting while driving has become because drivers feel an obsessive need to be two places at once. It fragments your focus and increases the likelihood of having a fatal accident. Every year in the United States, 1.6 million car crashes result from cell phone usage.[59] One study by the National Highway Transportation Safety Administration (NHTSA) concluded that texting while driving is six times more dangerous than driving while intoxicated.[60]

The cost of diverting our focus far outweighs the payoff. Digiphrenia causes anxiety and sleep deprivation. It also leads to decreased productivity and performance at work, and it negatively impacts relationships too.

Enough with all these facts—at least for the moment. I could use some oceanside time right about now.

Care to join me?

THE FUN?

You lie on a pristine beach listening to the waves smack against the sandy shore. Sipping your favorite cold beverage, the thought of your Boon creeps into your awareness. It feels close, so close you can almost taste it.

Lately, you've been distracted by the busyness of life. If only you could get laser-focused, you'd achieve your dream much faster. The past few weeks, the burnout and exhaustion have been kicking your butt—and sleep deprivation doesn't help. This ocean vacation is a welcome break.

Seabirds squawk off in the distance. You smile under the warmth of the sun. The gentle breeze brings with it the scent of the salty sea, and you doze off under the clear blue sky.

A while later, you awake and notice your skin is hot to the touch. The extended exposure to the sun produced a burn, but it's nothing a little aloe can't fix.

While daydreaming, you imagined achieving your Boon. It was the best mental trip you've taken in a long time—maybe the best of the last decade. You notice your skin again. It's on fire. The sunburn is worse than you imagined.

How long were you asleep? Minutes or hours? Judging from your arms and chest, you guess about three hours. A weird thought pops in your mind: You could have burned much faster if you focused the sun rays with a magnifying glass. By positioning the glass, you could burn a hole into nearly anything in a matter of three minutes, not three hours.

The difference? Focus!

Same sun. Same skin. But a very different result. The magnifying glass filters the sun's energy and intensifies the outcome at a much faster rate.

You take another sip of your beverage. It's warm now. You swallow hard while experiencing the unappealing taste. Still imagining your dream, an even weirder thought pops into your head. What if you had some kind of magnifying glass for your Boon? What if you could get that laser-focused in life?

Too bad there's no such thing.
Or is there?

BURNING A HOLE TO REACH YOUR BOON FASTER

Imagine having the ability to produce a similar effect regarding your dreams. What if you could

- leverage your focus to burn a hole right through any obstacle in the way of your Boon?

- amplify your energy and intensify your desired outcome at a much faster rate?

- shorten the gap between ideation and implementation?

With something called Focus Filters©, you can do all three. These filters help you achieve your goal—but in a fraction of the time. Use one filter, and you'll become an outlier. Use all three, and you'll tap into a superhuman ability to focus.

Today, I'll introduce you to the first Focus Filter. Then, over the next couple of days, you'll experience all three.

FOCUS FILTER #1—URGENCY

Humanity trades billions of messages back and forth every single day. Many of these messages go unnoticed. Add the word *urgent* and, suddenly, that same message gets special treatment. By its very definition, urgent means critical, requiring immediate action or attention.

Think about the term *urgent care*. In terms of priority, this type of facility often ranks under an emergency room but over a health care provider.

What's so *urgent* about the word urgent? Or, to put it another way, why does something urgent get extra special attention?

Urgency requires action because of a *baked-in deadline*. If the deadline is ignored, there's a price to pay in terms of health, finances, quality, or relationships. The factor that makes something urgent is the cost involved.

In our conversation about Unhackability, this isn't the first time you've heard the word "deadline." You encountered it on Day 6. Remember?

> Desire without a deadline is simply a pipe dream. It's easy to be fuzzy. Writing down a date makes it real. Even if you miss the date, it creates accountability. You know if you've made it or missed it.

I included the topic of deadlines in Day 6 to get you comfortable with the idea. Picking a deadline is important—similar to picking a destination for a road trip—without one, you're just going in circles.

But a deadline isn't enough. Just because you have a *destination* doesn't mean you have a *motivation*. What gets you moving in full force is *urgency*. Paying a penalty for missing your deadline injects a serious dose of motivation.

Consider the facts.

THE COST

In America, we have something called Tax Day. Unless there's a holiday, April 15 is the infamous day assigned for people to file their taxes. Most citizens would skip this event unless there were some penalty involved. In fact, 22% of people wait until the final two weeks to file their taxes.

What's crazy is that most people don't even have to *pay* money on that day. Instead, they're *owed* money in the form of a check. In fact, the average refund is more than $2,400, yet people still hate filing taxes because of the work involved.

For the 12% of taxpayers who file after the deadline, there's a potential penalty if they haven't paid enough in taxes. The IRS knows how to motivate taxpayers. It's called a clear deadline with a clear penalty.

Here are some truths about deadlines:

- About 1/3 of the population waits until the last minute.

- Deadlines with penalties create urgency.

- Without deadlines, very few things would get done.

These conclusions aren't surprising. However, something called Parkinson's Law is. Cyril Northcote Parkinson, the famous British historian and author, observed in 1955 that "work expands so as to fill the time available for its completion."[61]

"If you give yourself a week to complete a two hour task, then (psychologically speaking) the task will increase in complexity and become more daunting so as to fill that week. It may not even fill the extra time with more work, but just stress and tension about having to get it done."[62]

The amount of time which one has to perform a task is the amount of time it will take to complete the task. Think back to your school days. On the first day of class, did a teacher ever assign a project due at the end of the semester? If so, most students probably completed that assignment during the final week of the semester, maybe even the night before. However, in accordance with Parkinson's Law, the assignment took up mental, physical, and emotional energy the entire time, even if only subconsciously.

Students may not have been actually *working* on the project throughout the entire semester, but they carried the *weight* of the project from the moment their teacher assigned it to the moment the project was completed.

THE DREADED DEADLINE

This was my experience writing *Elixir Project*. The initial idea came to me in the wee hours of the morning on October 9, 2014. I awoke with the phrase "Elixir Project" and the idea for a fiction book.

So, what happened after I had the idea?

Nothing!

Nothing ever happens unless we have motivation. Thankfully, I had the note on my phone, and I didn't delete it. As I turned my focus to the idea, its importance slowly grew.

Months later, I thought more on the topic. Eventually, I even started writing the manuscript. Naively, I thought I'd finish in time to release it at the 2015 Igniting Souls Conference in October. Boy, was I wrong! I didn't even have half of it done.

Spring 2016 came around, and I was still struggling. I kept justifying my procrastination as "research time." Although I was doing *some* research, I kept delaying because I had no *urgency* to finish. I hadn't put any penalties in place. Besides, it kind of sounds important to say, "I'm working on my first novel." (Some people work on theirs for an entire lifetime.)

Everything changed on March 23, 2016. I found a brilliant editor—Julie Scheina—who read my proposal and agreed to work with me. I wanted to have *Elixir Project* books in hand at the 2016 Igniting Souls Conference in October. She was incredibly busy and couldn't begin editing my manuscript until June 22, 2016.

She sent a contract with the terms and payment amount. The hackable part of me pushed back when I read her contract.

Dear Kary,

I am pleased to have the opportunity to provide editorial services to you. This letter will serve as our agreement.

EDITORIAL SERVICES:
I will perform the following editorial services for your novel, *Elixir Project*, in manuscript form: editorial comments and line edits in the electronic manuscript file. The editorial services include a 30-minute follow-up phone call. The call will be scheduled upon request at a mutually convenient time no later than three months after delivery of the editorial notes.

DELIVERY:
I will receive a Word file of the complete manuscript via email by June 22, 2016, and I agree to provide the editorial notes on or before August 5, 2016. I will return the manuscript file via email. If the manuscript is not received by June 22, 2016, the project may need to be delayed or rescheduled. Please let me know as soon as possible if you do not anticipate being able to send the manuscript by this date.

FEES:
I estimate that the project will require 38–50.5 hours to complete, which equates to an estimated fee of XXXXX at the rate of $XX per hour. You agree to pay this fee. I will not exceed this estimate unless we mutually agree to do so. My estimate is based on the stated length of 75,000 words. If, upon review, the job appears to require more time to complete, I will contact you immediately so that we can reevaluate the project's requirements.

PAYMENT:
Payment will be made in two installments. Following signature, I will send you an initial PayPal invoice for XXXXX, approximately half of the estimated fee; this is payable by April 7, 2016. The remaining portion will be paid within 15 days after I complete the above services

and submit a second PayPal invoice. Should you decide to terminate the project before its completion, we agree that I will retain the initial payment and will be paid in full for all additional time I have spent on the project up to that point; I will return all materials to you immediately.

Interesting, I thought. This was the first time I had ever read such a contract. I wrote her and asked what happened if I failed to send her a complete draft by June 22, 2016. Subconsciously, I wanted to know if I had any wiggle room. She pushed back even more with a deadline and a penalty.

Deposits reserving editorial time are nonrefundable; this is because once we sign the agreement and I receive the deposit, I reserve the time in my schedule and decline conflicting requests accordingly. If a project is canceled, it's unlikely that I can recoup those lost hours.

Translation?

If I failed to deliver the manuscript, I'd lose my deposit and, more importantly, my place in line. I'd miss the conference date and my December 6, global release. Signing this contract would create the urgency I needed. It would give me the Focus Filter I had lacked up until now.

Since I wanted my time to count, I counted my time— March 23 to June 22. I signed the contract and paid the fee that day. I accepted the deadline and the penalty for missing the deadline.

Knowing my personality, I knew the manuscript was as good as done. There's no way I would throw all that money away. The cost created an immediate commitment.

THE BOON CYCLE

Completing the *Elixir Project* manuscript was not my Boon. However, it was a small but significant step that would lead me to my Boon. I knew without this manuscript, I couldn't create Elixir Project Experience (EPX), the course based on the book. Without Elixir Project Experience, I couldn't do an *Elixir Project* movie. And as best as I could tell, without an *Elixir Project* movie, I couldn't ignite one million souls. I call this chain of events a Boon Cycle©.

Boon Cycle
Small and Significant Steps That Lead to a Big Boon

My Boon Cycle
Elixir Manuscript ➡ EPX ➡ *Elixir* Movie ➡ Ignite One Million Souls

I knew there were other smaller steps within this process, but I only focused on my first one—signing the contract. Once that was signed, I focused on my next best step—turning the *Elixir Project* manuscript in to the editor on June 22, 2016. I knew this would create urgency and initiate a chain reaction. It all began by establishing a deadline and paying a penalty if I missed that deadline.

Think about your Boon.

1. What next best step do you need to take? (Don't overlook small steps. Small ones are significant ones.)

2. What chain reaction could result from taking this first step? (Think of three to five other outcomes that could happen as a result of this first action.)

Write your first Boon Cycle below. Don't focus on the exact number of steps—and don't focus on perfection. Take imperfect action instead. Remember, clarity only comes *after* you take action, not *before*.

My Boon Cycle

(smaller step)	(smaller step)	(smaller step)	(Boon)
_____ ➡	_____ ➡	_____ ➡	_____

CLOSE YOUR GAP DAY 13: ESTABLISH YOUR DEADLINE

Ready to apply urgency—the first Focus Filter—to your Boon? You'll leverage urgency when you establish a deadline and a subsequent penalty if you miss your deadline. You do this by signing a Boon Contract with yourself (similar to me signing a contract with my editor).

Because you are a person of integrity, once you sign this contract with yourself, you'll take your Boon more seriously. Share it with a trusted friend who will keep you accountable, and you'll increase your probability of becoming Unhackable. Just make sure your Boon Contract contains these three components:

1. **Action:** This action must be specific and measurable. For me, this was completing my *Elixir Project* manuscript.

2. **Delivery:** This must be a date. Be realistic but aggressive. Remember Parkinson's Law: If you give yourself too much time, the work will become too complex. A tighter deadline forces urgency and creates focus. You want "stretch" not "snap." (More on this in the next component—Flow.) For me, this

was three months to finish more than half of my novel.

3. **Penalty:** This penalty costs you something. Time? Money? Pride? You picked your Boon, so you need to pick your penalty. Be specific. For me, this was losing my deposit and, more costly than that, my place in line with the editor of my choice. This would delay my dream and my release date. It was something I wasn't willing to pay.

BOON CONTRACT

ACTION:

DELIVERY:

PENALTY:

UNDERSTOOD AND AGREED

NAME:

DATE:

Focus Filter Recap

Focus Filter #1 = Urgency

If I want my time to count, I must count my time.
Desire without a deadline is simply a pipe dream.

DAY 14

AGENCY:
Choose Your Inputs

*Your input determines your outlook. Your outlook determines
your output, and your output determines your future.*

—Zig Ziglar

Congratulations. You made it through one of the most
difficult days—Day 13. Accomplishing this feat says
a ton about your mental toughness. I'm proud of you
and your commitment toward becoming Unhackable.

Yesterday you leveraged urgency to complete your Boon
Contract. You're now ready for Focus Filter #2—Agency. Think
of agency as the place where you conduct business. Agency
recognizes your *ownership* of a particular space. Becoming
Unhackable is impossible until you realize you're responsible
for your own space.

Remember back to Day 3 and the difference between victims and victors? Victims lie in BED (Blame, Excuses, Denial)
while victors use their OAR (Ownership, Accountability,
Responsibility) to make progress.

Although we could examine every area of our lives related to agency, I'm only going to pick three. I've tried to use common, everyday examples to illustrate a point. The truth is, many of us get hacked in the smallest ways because we're not aware it's even happening. My hope is that, after today, you'll look at agency with a fresh perspective.

WAITING ROOMS BECOME WORKING ROOMS

Like most people, I get oil changes for my vehicles. For several reasons, I often get them done at the dealership. (If you don't go to a car dealership, don't get hung up on the details and miss the point. Many other examples parallel this one—doctor appointments, post office lines, dentist appointments, tire rotations, lines at the airport, etc. It's true any time or place that requires you to wait.)

The average oil change takes about sixty minutes. Most people walk into the waiting room and fiddle with a magazine or grab a bottle of water. Then, they sit in a seat and, rather than talking to a stranger, they stare at the blaring television screen from across the room.

No one dares to change the channel, so like lemmings, they choose to embrace the agency created for them by the car dealership. This is generally true for most waiting rooms. When we walk into some else's space, we let them *choose the inputs* for us.

I'm not better than anyone else in the room, but I do something completely different from most. Because my Boon has a deadline with a penalty, I don't waste time by consuming someone else's content or adopting someone else's agency. After I walk into the waiting room, I sit down and open up my laptop. I pop in my headphones and turn on my epic music playlist of choice found at YouTube Premium (commercial free), Focus@Will, or Brain.fm. This helps me create a space conducive to productivity, allowing me to dive in and work on my Boon. About an hour later, Eddie finds me in the waiting room and wakes me out of my flow state.

This is the same thing I do while waiting at airports, medical offices, and my kids' sports practices. While other people burn twenty minutes here or there by embracing someone else's agency, I create my own.

GET A PHD IN YOUR CAR

Many people get hacked during their commute to work or driving around town for a few errands. They figure it's only thirty minutes and justify flipping on talk radio or punching in a station to fill the time with music. By doing this, they embrace the station's agency. It's now directing their thoughts.

What's the big deal? They're only thoughts, after all. But in a short amount of time, thoughts become destinies. Notice the progression:

> Sow a *thought,*
> Reap an *action.*
> Sow an *action,*
> Reap a *habit.*
> Sow a *habit,*
> Reap a *character.*
> Sow a *character,*
> Reap a *destiny.*[63]

We tend to underestimate our thoughts and our time. Thirty minutes compounded over a week, a month, and a year become quite significant.

Business guru Brian Tracy reveals what's possible in our daily drive time.[64] The average person drives 12,000 to 25,000 miles per year, which works out to between 500 and 1,000 hours per year. If you prefer public transportation, the illustration still works.

You can become an expert in your field by simply listening to educational audio programs as you ride from place to place. Studies reveal something amazing about listening to audio programs while commuting. After three years, you could earn a doctorate level degree in your topic of focus. Our second Focus Filter—agency—is this powerful.

About ten years ago, I gave Audible (an audiobook subscription service) a try. As a father of three kids, I didn't have a ton of extra time to sit down and read books. Over the next sixty days, while running, driving, or mowing the lawn, I listened to a couple of audiobooks. I loved it so much I kept my subscription. For a low monthly fee, to this day, I still choose a new audiobook and listen to it each month. If I blow through those audiobooks, I'll buy more credits and keep on sharpening my mind. (For my list of recommended audiobooks visit UnhackableBook.com/free)

Many times, I choose a book that helps me research themes related to my latest Boon. Remember, listening to an audiobook and doing noncognitive tasks isn't multitasking. My productivity isn't hacked, and I can choose my inputs and create my agency.

Skip the Commercials and Make Money

The average person watches an hour of commercials every day. That's 365 hours a year. Not a big deal until we realize what 365 hours is worth. First, let's estimate the financial cost. Think about how much you'd charge someone if he or she hired you for an hour of consulting.

For some readers, this will be a difficult thought. They'll immediately bump up against self-limiting beliefs and think they or their time aren't worth anything. This is a different example of how we can hack ourselves: under-charging for our services.

If that's you, read one of my favorite quotes a few times and let it sink in.

Until you value yourself, you won't value your time. Until you value your time, you will not do anything with it.
—M. Scott Peck

If you don't struggle charging what you're worth, then what's your hourly rate? Is it $10, $100, $1,000, or $10,000? Now multiply that number by 365. If you chose an average rate for consulting of $100 an hour, then you burned $36,500 of billable hours per year watching commercials. Multiply that by seventy years and you've wasted over $2.5 million.

Worse than that, you chose to consume over 25,000 hours of other people's agency. Many of these messages were designed to tell you what you lack and why you need to purchase something else to complete you. It's hard to show up filled up when you've been told thousands of times that you're incomplete and lacking.

At our house, we choose to skip the commercials. This may mean starting a sports game thirty minutes late so we can zip past them. (For people without this technology, try muting the commercials.) Most houseguests think we're a little odd until they realize how much time they saved in an average sports game. At least 25% is filled with advertising and activities other than the game itself.

Do what you want. Your agency is yours, not mine or anyone else's. The point is that you should choose your inputs based upon your Boon, not on what sponsors decided in some marketing boardroom. Life is too short to waste.

CLOSE YOUR GAP DAY 14: CHOOSE YOUR INPUTS

For today's mission, I want you to do something incredibly simple. Although it may seem small, the action you take will pay big dividends. I'm inviting you to choose your inputs.

Pull out your calendar. Now, identify a time when you'll be in a waiting room, commuting across town, or watching

TV. Rather than letting someone else choose your agency for you, I want you to create your own.

In the space below, write out how you will choose your inputs. This may mean you record your TV show and skip the commercials. It may mean you download an audiobook or purchase a pair of earbuds or noise-canceling headphones. It may mean you plan ahead and bring your laptop, tablet, or book with you to the next waiting room. Or it may mean you download a podcast onto your smartphone for your next commute.

If you need a recommendation, start with the *Igniting Souls Podcast* if it fits your Boon.[65] Bottom line—exercise agency. Choose your inputs, don't let someone else choose them for you.

Today's takeaways:

1. Take an active role.

2. Choose your inputs.

3. Create your own agency.

I will choose my inputs by taking the following practical actions today:

Focus Filter Recap

Focus Filter #2 = Agency
The space I create will create me.
What I take in shapes what I put out.

DAY 15

ENERGY:
Allocate Your Attention

In the attention economy, anyone trying to connect with an audience must treat the user's time as the ultimate resource.

—Jakob Nielsen

Over the past two days, you've learned how to apply urgency and agency. You're now ready for Focus Filter #3—Energy. In case you need a quick reminder, here's a brief recap:

Focus Filter #1 = *Urgency*: Establish your deadline.
Focus Filter #2 = *Agency*: Choose your inputs.
Focus Filter #3 = *Energy*: Allocate your attention.

Remember, Focus Filters help you achieve a better outcome in a fraction of the time. Use one filter, and you'll become an outlier. Use all three, and you'll tap into your superhuman ability to

- leverage your focus to burn a hole right through any obstacle in the way of your Boon

- amplify your energy and intensify your desired outcome at a much faster rate

- shorten the gap between ideation and implementation

ENERGY IS EVERYTHING

A wise old man once told me, "At my age, success comes down to one thing—energy management." Since he was many decades older than me, who was I to argue? I didn't understand his statement at the time, but the older I get, the more I see his point. If we don't have energy, then we're done—and so is our Boon. We'll sit on the bench of life and fail to get in the game. *Urgency* and *agency* mean little if we lack the *energy* to take action. Whether you're running on full or on empty, there's always room for improvement in the area of energy.

The truth is, at the end of the day, many of us make comments about the way we feel. We say we're

- washed out
- flatlining
- fried
- maxed out
- fed up
- burnt out
- fatigued
- running on empty
- stressed out
- dragging
- worked to the bone
- drained
- depleted

Each of these statements reveals something about our energy level and our built-in limitations. We can't stay focused forever. Our attention eventually *subsides* due to overuse or *divides* due to multitasking

Sophie Leroy, a business school professor at the University of Minnesota, explains why in her article: "Why is it so hard to do my work? The challenge of attention residue when switching between work tasks."

She studied switch-tasking, an activity most of us do on a daily basis. In two experiments, Leroy found people are less productive when they constantly move from one task to another instead of focusing on one thing at a time.

> People need to stop thinking about one task in order to fully transition their attention and perform well on another. Yet, results indicate it is difficult for people to transition their attention away from an unfinished task and their subsequent task performance suffers.[66]

When we switch tasks, it's never a clean break because of attention residue. We still have thoughts and feelings committed to the original task. This practice leaks energy and drains our attention reserves at a much faster level. Compounding the issue, our productivity plummets due to the "cognitive load" we place upon ourselves.[67]

DECISION FATIGUE

As knowledge and information continue to grow, so does the number of daily choices we must make. According to *Psychology Today*, the average adult makes around 35,000 decisions a day.[68] As I shared earlier, a study done by Cornell University revealed that we make 226.7 daily decisions about food alone.[69]

The cost of making all these decisions produces something called decision fatigue. The quality of our decisions deteriorates over time. Similar to muscle becoming fatigued from an excessive period of exercise, our minds experience fatigue after an excessive period of decision-making.

To combat decision fatigue, some of the most successful people automate what they consider insignificant decisions so they can invest their limited attention on the bigger decisions. By reducing their daily decisions, they're able to exert greater focus and energy on the ones they deem most important. Rian Doris, co-founder of The Flow Research Collective, eliminated shopping at all stores for an entire year for this reason. Anytime we walk down an aisle, our subconscious brain must process thousands of micro-decisions.

For Mark Zuckerberg, former President Barack Obama, and the late Steve Jobs, this meant pre-deciding their wardrobe. According to a 2015 article in *Business Insider*, "They have to make tons of decisions all the time. And there's only so much mental energy in a given day." President Obama explained it this way: "Managing your life as a president requires that you cut away the mundane, frustrating decisions like deciding what to wear—which people around the world fret over. I'm trying to pare down decisions. I don't want to make decisions about what I'm eating or wearing. Because I have too many other decisions to make."[70]

About seven years ago, I decided to automate as many decisions in my life as possible. I wanted to save my creative energy for significant decisions, not trivial ones. Sometimes when I share about this in my keynotes, the audience thinks it sounds limiting. However, it's just the opposite. It's actually quite freeing.

This illustration sheds some light. When I was single and in college, an important decision oftentimes hacked my brain: Who would I marry someday? It literally shaped where I went, whom I talked to, and what I did. I constantly had the question burning in the back of my mind—*Is she the one?*

Because I didn't know the answer to the question, every single woman I met could have been *the one.* This was enough to overwhelm me, to say the least. However, in graduate school, I met and married Kelly, and that decision was then over.

By making that important decision over twenty years ago, I was free to move forward and focus on building our relationship. I also had more energy and attention to focus on other areas related to life and business.

Years later, authoring my OPUS helped even more.[71] Through this Deeper Path Process, I automated many more decisions and allocated my attention. I also protected my energy levels and increased my focus in the areas most important to me. (Go to KaryOberbrunner.com/OPUS to see my current OPUS.)

The truth is that life is going to try to hack you. Visit your email inbox for all the proof you need. You can bet the moment I got clear with my Boon and established a deadline, the hacks came from all directions. Life has a funny way of testing our commitment level. For example, I received this kind invitation:

> My consulting firm will be celebrating 10 years in business in October 2016! To commemorate the occasion, we are planning a 7 day tele-summit, and I would love for YOU to join me in the celebration as a guest speaker.

Even though some of these invitations seemed innocent enough, I already knew my answer. I didn't need to waste a second debating the issue. When your Boon is on the line, you don't have energy for getting hacked. Since time is a limited commodity, saying "yes" to an invitation like this is also saying "no" to my Boon. This was my reply:

> Honored by the invite.
> Unfortunately, I have to decline this amazing opportunity.
> I have too much on my plate with my forthcoming book, and I'm behind schedule. I wish you the best.

No is a powerful word. And according to American model, actress, and businesswoman Kathy Ireland, "No is a complete sentence."[72] Throughout her career, Ireland was asked to do many things out of alignment with her Boon. She developed a strong core and kept that strong core by allocating her attention and focusing her energy.

Billionaire and Berkshire Hathaway CEO Warren Buffett said, "The difference between successful people and really successful people is that really successful people say no to almost everything."[73] Focus Filter #3 works for supermodels and super investors alike.

CLOSE YOUR GAP DAY 15: ALLOCATE YOUR ATTENTION

For today's mission, I'd like you to start small. Rather than trying to automate every decision, start with one. I've discovered that automation is addicting—in a good way. When you see how powerful it is, you wonder why you didn't do it earlier. You soon identify all kinds of decisions you can automate.

In the space below, please identify one thing you can pre-decide in your life right now. Rather than spending your limited energy and attention on this decision, from now on, you'll already know the answer.

I'll give you two examples to help. One friend decided to work out every single day, no matter what. Another friend decided his wakeup time would be 6 a.m. every day of the week. Both friends eliminated hundreds of other decisions by pre-deciding these two.

Sometimes automating decisions is difficult. When I was in *Elixir Project* creation mode (writing, editing, publishing), I intentionally committed to no interviews. This meant pre-deciding I wouldn't be a guest on podcasts, radio, or TV.

This was a difficult decision. However, I knew all these little "yeses" would leak my energy. Knowing I have limitations,

I would reallocate all this attention and energy back toward *Elixir Project* and accomplishing my Boon.

Only when I completed the book could I consider interviews. Up until that point, this good thing (doing interviews) functioned as a bad thing (getting distracted) and a major hack to doing my dream.

Decision Automation
(What thing am I pre-deciding?)

Attention Allocation
(How will I reallocate that extra energy and attention toward my Boon?)

Focus Filter Recap

Focus Filter #3 = Energy
Where my attention goes, my legacy flows.
Attention is limited, and this limits me.

DAY 16

ALIGNMENT:
Align Your Assets

For when I am weak, then I am strong.

—The Apostle Paul

Welcome to the second half of this book—Day 16. By now, you know becoming Unhackable involves a certain type of pain.

This probably doesn't surprise you. What may surprise you is that some people actually think they can create a pain-free life. This is not only impossible but also ignorant.

People who live with eyes wide open understand the old saying—pain is inevitable; suffering is optional. Author and speaker Jim Rohn takes this concept of universal pain further, distinguishing between different types of pain:

> We must all suffer from one of two pains: the pain of discipline or the pain of regret. The difference is discipline weighs ounces while regret weighs tons.

I prefer the distinction made by Chet Scott, my friend and founder of Built to Lead. He labels these two pains as chronic pain and acute pain.[74]

Chronic Pain: This type of ache plagues most of the population most of the time. There is no resolution.

Acute Pain: This type of discomfort is intentional and specific. It leads to significant breakthroughs.

Most of us have been conditioned to think of pain as something that's bad. However, pain isn't good or bad—it simply is. Pain becomes good or bad based on what we do with it. Good pain is essential, and unless it's permitted (in many cases, even pursued), bad pain will triumph and have its way.

This is true in regard to physical pain. For example, take people who have a torn rotator cuff and live in chronic pain. For them to heal, they're going to first need to accept acute pain via a surgery and then even more acute pain via physical therapy. No one wants either form of acute pain. However, living the rest of your life with a torn rotator cuff is far worse.

The example holds true in regard to emotional pain too. In our context, people who get hacked choose lives of chronic pain. Contrast this with Unhackable people who choose lives of acute pain. Here's the difference:

Hackable | Bad Pain: *These people experience chronic pain in the form of long-term suffering that's ever-present and purposeless. This bad pain leads to a state of unproductive inaction and ultimately a type of serious injury or death (emotional, financial, relational).*

Unhackable | Good Pain: *These people experience acute pain in the form of short-term suffering that's intentional and purposeful. This good pain leads to productive action* *and, ultimately, a type of healing or resurrection (emotional, financial, relational).*

My friend Tom Ryan, the head coach of the Ohio State Buckeyes 2015 national championship wrestling team, has an interesting perspective on acute pain. He calls it chosen suffering, and he wrote the book on it—literally. In it, he expounds upon the concept:

> Chosen suffering is a foundation to growth and non-negotiable for progress. The chosen suffering I refer to the most is the kind that moves us to a healthy place of discomfort. It's the choice to push yourself past the point of fatigue—to a place it doesn't want to go—but you make it go anyway. This intersection is when growth begins to occur. If the love is strong enough, the suffering will be deep enough.[75]

Coach Ryan links suffering with love. Think back to your Boon. Do you love it enough that you're willing to suffer for it?

The ancients measured passion not by how much you loved something but by how much you were willing to suffer for it. This is why Jesus' crucifixion was called "the Passion." He didn't necessarily love pain. Rather, he loved what the pain would ultimately achieve. His cross became a critical step in the process of securing his crown.

The people I surround myself with choose suffering. They're intense, and they're committed to becoming Unhackable.

Choosing a life of full focus means turning toward pain rather than away from it. It means locking onto your fight, not other people's. And it means aligning your assets, not comparing yourself to everyone else. Unfortunately, this perspective is incredibly rare.

WISHING YOU WERE SOMEBODY ELSE

Have you ever found yourself poking around on the Internet and secretly wishing you were somebody else?

Maybe you saw a friend's online album and felt jealousy spring up inside. Or perhaps you stumbled across someone else's success and found yourself instantly envious. Our focus can easily shift from ourselves to others (but not in a good way).

We take an inventory of all their imagined assets ...

- a loving spouse
- more friends, fans, and followers
- a spacious house
- great genetics
- an influential network
- a beautiful family
- the perfect life

... and we lose sight of our own actual assets.

Can you relate?

Sure, we've always struggled with our neighbor's grass being greener than ours. But thanks to the Internet and social media, we now have access to billions of other people's backyards. If we're not prepared, we'll start focusing on others and get hacked in the process.

This reminds me of a counseling term I learned back in grad school—dissociation. Although there's a wide spectrum of characteristics, the major feature of all dissociative phenomena involves a detachment from reality. It's when you're physically present but mentally absent.

Often, people check out as a coping mechanism because their lives are full of chronic pain. They dissociate from their present circumstances and focus on someone or something else.

This defense mechanism allows people to distract themselves, even if only momentarily.

Labeling this practice *daydreaming* only minimizes the hack. Without embracing the acute pain of our present circumstances, we become spectators of our lives. We abdicate our power and embrace an existence where life happens to us. In this state of mind, we can't step closer to our Boon because our focus is on other people's assets, not our own.

SOMEONE ELSE WISHES THEY WERE YOU

Although it might be difficult to believe, right now, people are thinking about you. Perhaps even more surprising, they literally wish they were you. They're more in tune with your assets than you are.

When I realized this truth many years back, it forced me to stop focusing on others. It also helped me stop getting hacked. Wishing I was somebody else didn't move me closer to my Boon. Instead, it only widened the gap between where I was and where I wanted to be. By redirecting my focus, I closed the gap between myself and my Boon, immediately becoming more aware of my assets. With a little intentionality, I aligned these assets to work for me, not against me.

Thanks to this newfound clarity, I showed up filled up and took another step toward Unhackability.

CLOSE YOUR GAP DAY 16: ALIGN YOUR ASSETS

For today's mission, please engage with the following questions.

1. Up until now, have you found yourself wishing you were somebody else?

2. Up until now, who are the people you've wished you were?

3. Do you understand that this dissociative behavior has hacked you? If so, how so?

4. Do you realize right now someone else in the world wishes he or she were you?

5. List your assets—all those things or qualities you have that are valuable and useful.

6. Align your assets. Write out a sentence for each asset describing how it could help you with your Boon.

DAY 17

ATTRACTION:
Open Your Eyes

*Our eyes only see and our ears only hear
what our brain is looking for.*

—Dan Sullivan

S ensory overload. Maybe you've heard the term? Regardless, you've certainly experienced it. Wikipedia defines sensory overload this way:

> One or more of the body's senses experiences over-stimulation from the environment. There are many environmental elements that affect an individual. Examples of these elements are urbanization, crowding, noise, mass media, technology, and the explosive growth of information.[76]

I recently experienced sensory overload when I dropped my child off for a birthday party at an indoor amusement center complete with laser tag, video games, and roller skating. The blaring music, flashing lights, and disrupting smells from the concession bar combined to form an overwhelming experience.

Maybe you've confronted sensory overload at the big game, in a crowded concert, or while attempting to converse with your friend at the local sports bar surrounded by a dozen flat-screen TVs broadcasting ESPN.

These types of experiences cause some people to say, "I can't even hear myself think." This is a problem. The ability to think is deeply connected to becoming Unhackable—even Superman would agree.

THE WORLD IS TOO BIG

In a scene from *Man of Steel*, Clark Kent, who would one day become Superman, suffers from sensory overload. If you haven't seen the less-than-three-minute clip, you can find it on YouTube by searching for "Clark Kent the world is too big, Mom."

The scene begins with nine-year-old Clark sitting at a desk in a classroom. Pencils flash across the screen—an American flag waves ever-so-slightly. With her back to the class, his teacher scribbles on a chalkboard. We hear her finish her question, "… when Kansas became a territory?"

She turns and faces the young children expecting to hear an answer.

"Clark?"

No response. Clark looks frantically throughout the room, eyes darting here and there. His breathing quickens.

"Are you listening, Clark? I asked if you could tell me who first settled Kansas."

Clark can't focus. His mind races. Because of his X-Ray vision and super-sensitive hearing, he picks up every tiny sound—fingers tapping, hearts pumping, clocks ticking.

The concerned teacher asks, "Are you all right, Clark?"

He covers his ears from the over-stimulation and bolts out of the classroom, attempting to shut out the noise. In desperation, he ducks into a janitor's closet and locks the door. Cowering in a corner against a mop bucket, he blocks out the sounds with his hands. Hanging his head, he closes his eyes, struggling to recreate a place of solace.

His teacher runs after him and bangs on the door.

"Leave me alone," he begs.

Time passes.

The teacher shouts, "Open the door. I've called your mother."

Martha Kent arrives a few minutes later and tries a different tactic. She leans against the door and says, "Sweetie. How can I help you if you won't let me in?"

"The world's too big, Mom," Clark says.

"Then make it small," his mom advises. "Focus on my voice. Pretend it's an island out in the ocean. Can you see it?"

Clark closes his eyes, shutting out every other input. After a few moments, Clark opens his eyes again and says, "I see it."

Martha Kent lifts her chin and smiles slightly, this time with a twinge of hope. She offers kind, direct instruction. "Then swim towards it, honey."

The doorknob turns slowly, and Clark cautiously exits the closet.

WE'RE NOT IN KANSAS ANYMORE

Life is far from the agricultural space our ancestors experienced generations before. Peace, quiet, and the ability to hear yourself think are luxuries a city can't buy. Suburbs can't afford them either. Lawns need mowing. Leaves need blowing. And the trees could use some tender love from screaming chainsaws.

It's time we all learned how to tap into our superhuman ability to focus, even those of us who weren't born superheroes. Because of biology, we already have this ability hard-wired into our brains. It's called the Reticular Activating System (RAS), and understanding how to use it is necessary for becoming Unhackable.

According to the *Textbook of Clinical Neurology*, your RAS is "a network of neurons located in the brain stem that project anteriorly to the hypothalamus to mediate behavior, as well as both posteriorly to the thalamus and directly to the cortex for activation of awake, desynchronized cortical EEG patterns."[77]

Since that's jargon for most of us, I prefer a basic definition. Your RAS is a set of connected nuclei in the base of your brain that prevents information overload.

Think back to the *Man of Steel* clip. Clark Kent was on the verge of mental meltdown because his RAS didn't filter out all of the competing stimuli. As a result, he experienced information overload. If we didn't have a RAS filter, you and I would too. Instead, we can feel grateful we were designed with this essential biological masterpiece.

Here's why. The conscious brain processes about forty bits of information a second. That might sound impressive until we realize the subconscious brain processes over 11 million bits of information a second.[78] That estimate is extremely conservative. In his book *Evolve Your Brain*, Dr. Joe Dispenza says that "the brain processes 400 billion bits of data every second."

Experts believe we each have "approximately 100 billion cells in the brain, each with connections to thousands of other brain cells. Equipped with this many processors, the brain could be capable of executing as many as 100 billion operations per second."[79]

What does all of this have to do with becoming Unhackable? The short answer is everything. Let's get incredibly practical with the remainder of Day 17 to discover *why* your RAS filter is important and *how* we can leverage it to our advantage.

In my book *Elixir Project*, I unpack it further:

"RAS stands for Reticular Activating System. Your RAS filter is at the base of your brain, and it sifts through all incoming stimuli. It decides what sensory input to address and which to ignore. It ignores more than ninety-nine percent, and the tiny

part it focuses on deals with one of four elements: surprise, danger, changes in the environment, or fear."

"Or...?" Tilda pushes.

"Or it focuses on what you tell it to focus on, like in the case of Pallas, the idea of a red car," Kiran says.

"Those red cars were there all along. You didn't see them because you weren't focused on them," Phoebe explains. "We now know the conscious mind processes somewhere between forty and two hundred bits of information per second. However, the unconscious mind processes billions and billions of bits of information in that same amount of time. If there were no filter, your conscious mind would experience information overload and literally go into meltdown mode."

"Does this make sense?" Tilda asks.

"I'm kind of getting it," Pallas replies.

"Think about what you did regarding the red car," Tilda says. "You set your mind on it. And once you consciously made that decision, your unconscious mind did the rest of the work. It sifted through billions and billions of bits of information to find what you told it to look for—in this case, a red car. Some call this phenomenon your mind's eye."

FRIEND OR FOE?

Your RAS filter is neutral. It can be your worst enemy or your best friend. If you tell it to look for all the roadblocks, barriers, and objections, then your brain will do a brilliant job of gathering all the information that proves why your Boon won't work. As a result, you'll stop before you start.

Ignorant people attribute this phenomenon to the "Law of Attraction." Informed people attribute this phenomenon to the RAS filter.

Napoleon Hill, the author of *Think and Grow Rich*, had plenty to say on this topic. He said, "Our minds become magnetized with the dominating thoughts we hold in our minds ... these 'magnets' attract to us the forces, the people, the circumstances of life which harmonize with the nature of our dominating thoughts."[80]

Ironically, our RAS becomes our reality. If we see ourselves as failures and losers, we repel successful people. After all, why would successful people want to partner down?

But the opposite is true too. If we see ourselves as winners and worthy, then we attract successful people. They want to partner up because they believe we are a worthwhile investment.

Said another way, you don't get what you want—you get who you are. And who you are is a direct result of your focus. As the ancient text says, "For as he thinks within himself, so he is."[81] If you want *to be* different, you need *to see* differently.

Bottom line:

Your RAS = Your Reality

This excerpt from *Elixir Project* will provide some missing clues:

> *"The main premise is this: Don't focus on attracting into your life what you want. Instead, focus on what's already all around you. Just open your mind's eye and you'll see everything you need to implement your idea."*

> *"Sounds amazing," Phoenix comments. "Any drawbacks?"*

"Of course there are always drawbacks," Kiran says arrogantly. *"If you believe you're an idiot per se—a fact for most of you—then your RAS filter works overtime finding evidence to back up that belief. It will ignore the billions of reasons why you're brilliant and focus on the few that suggest you're not. Once this happens, you need to reset your mind with the idea that you're brilliant. When you do, then your RAS filter kicks into overdrive, scavenging for all the evidence to support the belief that you're brilliant."*

"The mind is powerful," Tilda says. *"It shapes what we believe and dictates the version of truth we tell ourselves."*

FILTER FORMULA

By now, on Day 17, you probably have some fears about your Boon. This isn't a bad thing. Fear is simply an indicator that you haven't been here before. It alerts you to the fact that you're stepping into new territory. But fear is also like a fork in the road. It gives you a choice. You can either fortify your fears and become set in your ways or fortify your faith and invite change.

FEAR + RAS FILTER = FORTIFIED FEAR
FAITH + RAS FILTER = FORTIFIED FAITH

Remember, you'll always fortify what you focus on. Neuropsychologist Donald Hebb said it another way: "Neurons that fire together, wire together." He discovered that pathways in the brain are formed and reinforced through repetition.[82]

If you don't want obstacles, then don't focus on them. If you want opportunities instead, focus on them. Regardless of your choice, you will become a stronger version of yourself, defined either by fear or faith.

CLOSE YOUR GAP DAY 17: OPEN YOUR EYES

For today's mission, you have the opportunity to see life differently by resetting your RAS filter. List five things you are going to *start* looking for in life:

1.

2.

3.

4.

5.

List five things you are going to *stop* looking for in life:

1.

2.

3.

4.

5.

How will resetting your RAS filter move you closer to your Boon?

DAY 18

AMPLIFICATION:
Amplify Your Impact

Whenever you see a successful business, someone once made a courageous decision.

—Peter F. Drucker

I f you do a Google image search with the phrase *messy computer desktop*, you might be tempted to have a panic attack when you see the results—literally. Cortisol, the stress hormone, shoots through your bloodstream whenever you feel overwhelm and alarm. For me, an excessively cluttered computer screen initiates the release of this particular hormone, and it's not pretty.

This undesirable feeling appears to be somewhat universal. In fact, one magazine posted an article titled "These Horrifyingly Messy Desktops Will Give You So Much Anxiety." The writer showcases pictures of desktops so stress-inducing that one comment reads, "This horror made me scream & roll fetus position."[83]

It's not only desktops, though. The problem is just as bad and the stress just as high with too many browser tabs and too

145

many open windows. Do another Google image search, this time with the phrase *too many browser tabs*. These image results could push someone over the edge—certainly if you're the person who's trying to keep track of all those open windows.

Do you feel a twinge of stress when you see the plethora of icons, windows, tabs, and programs? Your computer feels the same way. All of these open activities sabotage productivity.

As you know, every computer has a limited amount of RAM. If too many things are going on at once, the computer's impact is severely hacked.

In an article on *Techlicious,* Natasha Stokes shares "15 Reasons Why Your Computer Is Slow."[84] Ironically, many of the reasons are also why humans get hacked. I'll list six of them. Notice the parallels:

1. *You have too many startup programs*

2. *Your hard drive is failing*

3. *Your hard drive is 95% full*

4. *Your browser has too many add-ons*

5. *You're running too many programs at once*

6. *Too many browser tabs are open*

Essentially, the computer is trying to do too many things at once. Sound familiar? Because of this, Stokes gives a somber warning:

Doing a trillion things at once is exactly why we have computers but, at some point, your little bundle of artificial intelligence is going to falter. Your computer's ability to run multiple programs at the same time hinges in part on its RAM (random access memory) ... but if the demands of the open programs are outstripping your computer's memory and processing power, you'll notice a slowdown.

Too many open tabs don't help. In our desire not to forget something or not to miss out, we keep windows open and end up sacrificing the overall performance of the machine.

> If you're in the dozens of open tabs camp … your browser is likely hogging far more than its fair share of RAM. "When you open a new browser tab, it's saved in RAM. If you have only a little bit of RAM left free, you run out of room for processing everything that is active, so the computer slows down."

THE IMPACT OF OPEN WINDOWS

Although humans are different than computers, in some ways, we're not. Focus Filter #3 revealed that, like a computer's RAM, we have limited energy. As a result, we must be intelligent about allocating our attention. Automating decisions will conserve some of this energy, but it's still not enough.

The majority of us have way too many programs running in the background when we start up in the morning. We may not consciously think about all the tasks we need to do, the places we need to go, and the people we need to see, but all of that seeps into our subconscious. I call these unresolved issues *open windows*, and the weight of them severely impacts our overall performance.

Despite our best intentions, with all these open windows, we can't show up filled up. Actually, we're lucky to show up at all. We feel empty before we begin and spread too thin before we even start. As a result, our impact suffers.

DITCH DELAYING

Perhaps you've heard author Jack Canfield's advice when it comes to decision making. He suggests one of four responses:

1. Do It

2. Delegate It

3. Delay It

4. Dump It

There's only one problem with his advice—the *delay it* option. The Unhackable Impact Equation© reveals why it's a terrible idea.

UNHACKABLE IMPACT EQUATION©

DO IT ⟶ *You do it!*

DELEGATE IT ⟶ *Somebody else does it!*

DUMP IT ⟶ *Nobody does it!*

DECIDED = CLOSED WINDOW → AMPLIFY IMPACT

DELAY IT ⟶ *Who does it?*

UNDECIDED = OPEN WINDOW → INHIBIT IMPACT

When we *do it, delegate it,* or *dump it,* we close a window. Either we're doing it, somebody else is doing it, or nobody is doing it. These three responses require a decision.

Unhackable people always make decisions. Decisions are powerful because they signify closure. Closure is permanent, hence the word *decide*. Decide is one of my favorite words because it comes with a cost—a death, in fact.

In my book *The Deeper Path*, I describe why:

The etymology of the English word *decide* comes from the Latin word *decidere*, which means "to cut off," and its cousin, the related Latin word *caedere*, which means "to cut" or "to kill." Our English word *homicide* comes from this same Latin word, *caedere*.

So when we make a decision, we are literally "killing our options." We are cutting off the chance to remain open to other possibilities.[85]

In a strange way, whenever we make a decision, we experience a type of loss. Many of us try to avoid making decisions altogether. We think we're preventing ourselves from feeling loss. However, we fail to realize not making a decision is actually a decision in and of itself. We will never be confronted with that exact same opportunity in that exact moment ever again. By choosing not to decide, we are actually choosing to stay exactly where we are. Indecision doesn't solve a problem. It only prolongs pain.

Dan Ariely, the author of *Predictably Irrational*, explains the psychology behind indecision. "Closing a door on an option is experienced as a loss, and people are willing to pay a price to avoid the emotion of loss."[86]

Hacked people rarely make decisions. As a result, they leave many windows open. Indecision requires that our subconscious keep expending energy and attention on unresolved issues. As with a computer, these open windows drastically reduce our overall performance and productivity. Open windows hack our focus by introducing an endless number of distractions.

CLOSED WINDOWS

I do a powerful exercise with some of my coaching clients called Closed Windows. I'll explain the Four-Step Process by referencing a recent client's experience.

Closed Window Process

1. **Identify:** Using sticky notes, she wrote down her unresolved issues, one per note. These were issues that were undecided and running in the background of her mind.

2. **Arrange:** She spread out the twenty notes to see them all at once. She realized these open windows were hacking her. Subconsciously, she was spending incredible amounts of attention and energy trying to deal with these issues.

3. **Decide:** She wanted to amplify her impact, so she needed to close some windows. She decided to put these notes in one of three categories: *do, delegate,* or *dump.*

4. **Delay:** One open window was so big, I recognized it would be difficult for her to decide in our session which action to choose. Because of this, I let her delay—momentarily.

In "big window" situations like this, I give a rare seventy-two-hour pass. She was struggling with whether to publish her book or not. She'd already invested a large amount of time trying to write it. As her coach, I felt the energy from her internal conflict. Her head was telling her one thing and her heart another. Although we could have forced the decision, I gave her the seventy-two-hour option. This means that a decision is so big, you give your conscious brain permission to grind on it for three days (maximum).

In those seventy-two hours, you can pray. You can fast from media or food. You can journal or take a walk outside. In this extreme case, you recognize the weight of the decision and its implications, and you choose to exert all your attention and energy to make this particular decision. This option is incredibly rare.

All of my client's other open windows had a very short timeline. Once she had identified and arranged them, she made all nineteen decisions in about thirty minutes.

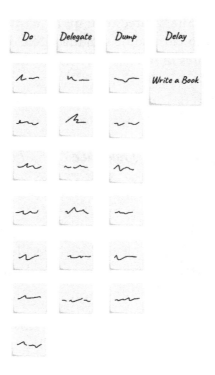

As we had agreed in advance, exactly seventy-two hours after our session ended, she sent me an email telling me her decision about her book—the one decision she was allowed to *delay*. She closed the window by deciding to *dump* it.

In my gut, I felt this was the right decision for her. She would have delayed endlessly because she feared closure on a dream she'd begun years ago.

The seventy-two-hour option forced her to close the window and *dump* the book. For most other clients, I would have encouraged them to *do* the book and close other windows to create additional energy and attention for their book. But for her, I knew her heart wasn't in it—at least for now.

In her email below, you can see that after dumping the book, she immediately opened a new window and decided to do something else noteworthy instead.

⊠ Inbox   — ↗ ✕

to Kary

Subject: Closed Window

Good afternoon!

Again, thank YOU for an amazing coaching session Friday!

I am letting you know that the book is a closed window.

I am also opening the ▮▮▮▮▮▮▮▮▮▮ window back up as it is in Columbus this year.

Everything else has stayed the same and I just crafted a newsletter that is better connected to the work that I am doing in another area. A great take-away from Friday for me was that I need to not always come up with NEW content, but force my tribe to go DEEP with current content they are implementing. Of course I always "knew" this, but didn't live it. Just implementing this one idea helps to close windows. wow...

Thanks Kary!

▮▮▮▮▮▮▮

This is in harmony with the laws of nature. Empty space is always filled with something else. Just think back to your first apartment or house if you need any proof. In no time, those empty spaces get filled. This is also true about our minds. By closing open windows, we often make more space for our Boon.

CLOSE YOUR GAP DAY 18: AMPLIFY YOUR IMPACT

It's time for you to amplify your impact. Please follow these steps:

1. **Identify:** Using the space below (or sticky notes), write down your unresolved issues. These are all the undecided issues running in the background of your mind. Don't rush the process. If you give yourself a few minutes, they will keep coming to the surface.

These could be big or small issues. Write them all down.

2. **Arrange:** Look at these open windows all at once. Spread them out on a table or wall. Do you realize they are hacking you? Do you know, subconsciously, you are spending incredible amounts of attention and energy trying to deal with these issues?

3. **Decide:** To amplify your impact, you need to close these windows—all of them. Decide to put these open windows into one of the three categories below.

4. **Delay**: If there's one decision too important to decide now, consider delaying it for seventy-two hours. Only do this for *one* open window—if you absolutely must—and only do it if your head and heart are in conflict. Otherwise, decide to close all windows now.

5. If you delay one of your decisions, you must come back in seventy-two hours or less with a clear decision. This is an honor system. If you do this, choose to spend the next seventy-two hours focused on making the best decision you can make at this moment.

THE OPEN WINDOW

I'm delaying this decision for the next seventy-two hours:

I have come back seventy-two hours later and decided to:

Do It ☐   *Delegate It* ☐   *Dump It* ☐

With all these windows you closed, you may have freed up some space for your Boon. Although this is not always the case, has anything new come to your awareness you can now *do* or *delegate*? If so, please list them now.

DAY 19

ACTIVATION:
Activate Your DIET

Perfection is achieved, not when there is nothing more to add,
but when there is nothing left to take away.

—Antoine de Saint-Exupery

Welcome to the final day of the Focus module. On this path to becoming Unhackable, whether you know it or not, you're changing in a number of ways, the most significant being how you see yourself—your identity.

As I've said before, this is in line with one of my favorite quotes by Anaïs Nin. She said, "We don't see things as they are, we see them as we are."[87]

Self-image affects everything. It's more important than your net worth and your networks. More powerful than your associations and your intelligence. It even influences the way you see your Boon. The truth is we don't get what we want in life; we get who we are. And who we are is determined by how we see ourselves.

Unfortunately, most people see themselves as consumers. Another large percentage of the population see themselves as critics. But only a small minority see themselves as creators.

So, which are you? The Focus Framework© may help fill in some missing pieces.

FOCUS FRAMEWORK©

IDENTITY	INPUT	OUTPUT
CONSUMER	No filter (Everything Goes)	Nothing
CRITIC	No filter (Nothing Goes)	Nothing
CREATOR	Filter (Some Things Go)	One Thing

Here's a breakdown:

Identity

This is how you see yourself. Your identity influences your actions. Runners run. Writers write. Swimmers swim. And in our context, consumers consume, critics criticize, and creators create.

Input

This is what you take in. Notice consumers and critics don't have any filters. They don't have any focus either. Consumers consume everything. Critics criticize everything and everyone. Creators, on the other hand, have a filter. As a result, they only accept the things that help them achieve their Boon.

Output

This is what you put out. Notice consumers don't put out anything. They're too busy consuming. Critics don't put out anything either. They're too busy criticizing. Creators are the exception. They put out one thing: their Boon.

Up until reading this book, how *did* you see yourself?

    Consumer ☐   *Critic* ☐   *Creator* ☐

With your new awareness, how do you now see yourself?

    Consumer ☐   *Critic* ☐   *Creator* ☐

THE NEED TO DIET

A few months back, I overheard a woman boasting about the number of books she'd read over the past year (more than one per week). She also mentioned subscribing to dozens of blogs and podcasts, attending conferences, purchasing products, and enrolling in many courses.

The other people hearing her boasts shrunk back. According to their comments, they weren't consuming half as much content as her, not even 10%. The self-limiting beliefs and doubts were written all over their faces.

If sheer volume of content were the true sign of success, then we should all drop everything and go binge. But content alone never helped anyone succeed. Knowledge isn't power. The right use of knowledge—also called wisdom—is true power.

As you might expect, this consumer who boasted to everyone around her wasn't creating anything of her own. She didn't have time to!

Focusing on volume at the expense of depth only ensures a shallow level of success. The truth is, most of us would experience massive benefits, personally and professionally, if we went on a DIET.

Don't worry. It has nothing to do with *calorie* restriction. Rather, it has everything to do with *content* restriction. I call it the Information DIET. I went on the Information DIET about ten years ago because I wanted to start winning even more. I knew I needed a change.

So, why do we need a DIET? Think back to Day 13— Urgency. Remember, there's more information produced every two days than all the information ever created from the beginning of time until 2003. In other words, if you're going to play the volume game, you'll lose every day.

Have you ever stood in front of the cupboard or refrigerator looking for something to eat when you're not even hungry? If so, you're not alone. We like to consume food when we're bored, confused, overwhelmed, or uninspired.

Guess what? We do the same thing with content. When we feel bored, confused, overwhelmed, and uninspired, we often distract ourselves by consuming more content.

The problem is most people aren't even applying 1/10 of what they already know. More content gives us the illusion of accomplishment. We rationalize that we're doing something, but simply shoveling in more content only leaves us feeling guilty, lazy, and undisciplined.

Ten years ago, I made a commitment not to consume content unless I had a pre-established purpose. I took James Allen's words to heart: "Until thought is linked with a purpose, there is no intelligent accomplishment."[88]

I decided not to go to the cupboard (in this case, the Internet) and consume empty calories. Instead, I determined to do the tough work before I "ate." I identified my purpose for consuming the content first.

Then I committed not to consume another piece of content until I applied what I'd consumed. This drastically reduced my intake, and it also forced me to move toward my Boon at a much faster pace.

ELEMENTS OF THE INFORMATION DIET

Most people would be amazed how much time they'd save if they were selective about the content they consumed. Obviously, I'm not suggesting we stop consuming altogether. I use the Information DIET as my filter.

If you apply this formula, you'll save a minimum of ten hours per week for the rest of your life. It's that powerful.

- **D** = *Determine* where you want to go.

- **I** = *Identify* who's getting the results you want.

- **E** = *Eliminate* all the empty calories.

- **T** = *Turn* your focus only after squeezing and applying every last drop of value.

CLOSE YOUR GAP DAY 19: ACTIVATE YOUR DIET

Now, it's your turn. You've already done most of the work in previous daily missions. This is the benefit of identifying your Boon—you already know where you're headed.

- **D** = *Determine* where you want to go.

Write your Boon:
(Celebrate the fact that you probably have more clarity today than you did on Day 2 when you first picked your Boon.)

- **I** = *Identify* who's getting the results you want.

I identify one person I want to focus on. Then, for the next season of life, I mine this person for all the content he or she is willing to give. There's a danger in consuming content from ten different people with ten different success models. Most people ignorantly blend these models together and then wonder why implementing this blend in their life didn't work.

The problem is that many of these success models are unique and often even opposed to one another. Blending them together is a recipe for failure.

It's similar to throwing ten different foods in a blender and drinking it. Imagine combining pizza, pickles, cheese, grapefruit, nuts, brownies, ice cream, steak, avocados, and sushi. Yuck! This unappealing example is true for content and calories alike. Stop blending your influencers together.

Identify one person you need to study:

- **E** = *Eliminate* all the empty calories.

Consuming empty calories hacks us. It's distracting, and it sucks up our limited energy and attention. This is why I'm committed to deleting, unsubscribing, and filtering.

There are dozens of tricks and tips to filter out empty calories in opposition to your Boon. Sure, it might take a little work in the beginning, but remember why you're doing this. Unhackability doesn't happen by accident—only intentionally.

I know people who filter their Facebook News Feed. Using tools, they prevent unwanted posts with certain keywords from showing up on their feed or wall.

List all your empty calories below. Commit to eliminating them now or within the next twenty-four hours:

- **T** = *Turn* your focus only after squeezing and applying every last drop of value.

When he was just a penniless tramp, Edwin C. Barnes met the great Thomas Edison. He offered to sweep floors just to be near to Edison. He knew proximity was power, and he mined Edison for decades, arguably his entire career. Edison kept learning, so Barnes kept listening. Eventually, Barnes became a distributor of Edison's inventions and later his business partner. Most people moved on, but they quit too early and missed the treasure. Barnes stayed and reaped a rich reward.[89]

Sometimes, you do need to move on and learn from someone else. My friend the coach, Tom Ryan, did this in his wrestling career. Although he earned a generous scholarship from Syracuse to wrestle, after a couple of years, he left it all to walk onto Iowa—the #1 team in the nation—without any guarantees. He risked the safety and security of a locked-in spot at Syracuse for a chance of learning from the best coach in the world, Dan Gable, the Olympic gold medalist. He knew this was the only path if he wanted a realistic shot of achieving his Boon.

Commit to staying the course with the person you identified above. Remain with him or her until you've mined everything you can. And while consuming their content, make a commitment to keep on creating too.

I will turn my focus only after squeezing and applying every last drop of value:

Yes ☐   No ☐

PART 4

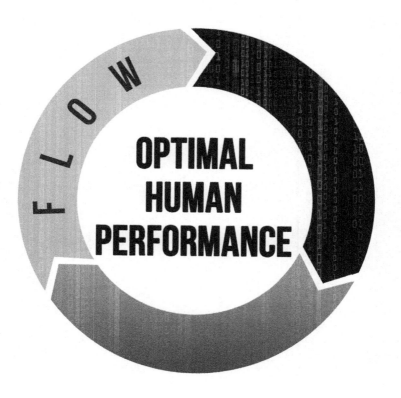

DAY 20

CHARACTERISTICS:
Optimize Your Performance

*Flow is the mental state of operation in which a person
performing an activity is fully immersed in a feeling of
energized focus, full involvement, and enjoyment
in the process of the activity.*

—Mihály Csíkszentmihályi, *Flow*

Welcome to the third and final component in the
Unhackable Circle©. We started our journey with
the first component—Idea (specifically Flawless
Idea Anatomy). We then explored the second component—
Focus (specifically Deliberate Magnetic Focus). And now,
it's time to unpack Flow—specifically the Optimal State of
Human Performance.

Although flow has been around since the beginning of
humanity, thanks to advances in science and technology, it is
now front and center in almost every conversation related to high
performance, heightened productivity, and super achievement.

It's also called "bullet time." In flow, the game slows down
long enough for you to influence the outcome. While the rest

of the population simply reacts to life, you have a way to steer it. You experience near-perfect decision-making, where your inner critic goes silent and you no longer self-edit.

For those new to flow, these benefits seem otherworldly or at least hyped-up—something we'd find in a Hollywood script. But physiologically speaking, it's fundamental neurobiology, and it's what happens to your prefrontal cortex when you're in flow.

Although *Elixir Project* is labeled science fiction, when writing my novel, I meticulously researched many details related to flow. My studies spanned from the work of Mihály Csíkszentmihályi (often referred to as the architect of flow) to Steven Kotler (award-winning journalist, executive director of the Flow Research Collective, and one of the world's leading experts on high performance).

In *Elixir Project*, I wanted to introduce the world to flow via story. The brief excerpt below unpacks flow in a conversational manner:

> *"The rest of the day is yours, clerics. Use the time to recover. Focus on eating, sleeping, and resting because you'll need your strength. Flow Verdict begins tomorrow at six a.m."*

> *Flow? A dozen or more times over the past few years during dinner discussions, Cai has ranted and raved about the newest breakthroughs in Flow.*

> *"But this is different," Cai told me. "Flow is optimal human performance. In Flow states, we're five hundred percent more productive. We can shut out distraction, gather more information, and experience enhanced pattern recognition. Flow gives us the ability to make faster connections between ideas."*

. . .

Phoenix jumps in immediately. "How is that even possible? We've reached moments of Flow in game-time situations, but sustaining five hundred percent sounds like science fiction."

"Correction, dearie—science fact," Kiran says. "In Flow, your brain releases five of the most potent neurochemicals on the planet: norepinephrine, dopamine, endorphins, anandamide, and serotonin. Each plays a critical role. Norepinephrine increases heart rate, attention, and emotional control. Dopamine blends nicely with your RAS filter, allowing you superhuman focus that leads to pattern recognition and skill-enhancing abilities. Endorphins increase your threshold for withstanding physical, emotional, and mental discomfort."

"We're not talking about a little pain, either," McNultey says.

"Most people have experienced Flow without even knowing it," Phoebe says. "Long-distance runners call it runner's high. Musicians call it playing in the pocket. Football players call it being in the zone."

Kiran continues to unpack the final two neurochemicals. "Anandamide elevates mood, relieves pain, and augments lateral thinking—your ability to link contrasting ideas together."

That's what I need. The ability to recognize how all these pieces fit together.

"And serotonin is the fifth and final one," Kiran explains. "It helps you stick with a task in spite of pain."

"Sounds powerful. So what's ELIXIR's role, then?" Damon asks.

"By monitoring your brains, we've discovered that part of what makes you four clerics unhackable is your propensity

for Flow," Kiran says. "Although the general population has varying levels of Flow potential, yours is limitless."

"What are you saying?" I ask.

"That we've never seen anything like it before," Phoebe clarifies. "It's quite simply herculean—and if it can be harnessed and reproduced, you'll be the very definition of Optimal Human Performance. We're going to punch the pedal to see what you're made of."

"Lucky us," Karme says sarcastically.

"Time will tell that," McNultey laughs.

"But helmets will help," Tilda says. "We'll use them to monitor your Flow state inside the Verdict."

I wonder what new skills they shot into our psyche this time. Then again, based on the other two Verdicts, maybe I don't want to know.

"Clerics, when you're in a Flow state you experience near-perfect decision-making—absorbing information, synthesizing it, and then integrating it," Tilda says. "You're so focused in the moment you're not even aware of yourself or your limitations. Your inner critic goes silent and you no longer self-edit."

I can't imagine a time where I no longer self-edit. My life is one constant judgment. How do I look? How do I sound? What do they think? Is this right?

"There's a dark side to Flow, though," Tilda cautions. "There's a chance you won't want to come back."

I lean in, worried.

"Don't underestimate these five neurochemicals. Ask any addict," Tilda continues. "And don't get so caught up in the Deep Now you forget the true reason we sent you in. You're in there because we need the ELIXIR vaccine."

Her words snap me back to reality. If we fail—or if we fail to come back, humanity pays the ultimate price.

"So when do we start?" Damon asks.

WHY FLOW IS SO POWERFUL

When you're in flow, something unique takes place to your prefrontal cortex. Essentially, it goes dark. According to Kotler:

> The extrinsic system turns off, and the intrinsic system takes over. It's an efficiency exchange. During focused attention, your brain has a fixed energy budget. It's 2% of your body weight but uses 20% of your energy. It's a big energy hog. When energy is needed for concentration and attention, the brain performs an efficiency exchange. It flips from conscious processes when it's slow to very energy intensive, time conscious processes. In flow ... one of the reasons it's so strange, because you're essentially watching your self-conscious mind process reality; and normally you never get to see that.[90]

Outside of flow, we *always* self-edit. The only segment of the population that doesn't is babies. They don't blush because they're born unaware. Slowly, over time, they become self-aware—and when they do, the judgment starts.

It's quite common for people to admit that they are their own worst critic. However, by analyzing everything we think, say, feel, and do, we remove ourselves from the present moment. Productivity halts and stress abounds.

This is why humans often crave activities where they can let their minds go. We enjoy the neurochemicals released in flow—and if we can't experience them naturally, some seek them artificially through fabricated chemicals and illegal drug use.

But not all turn to pharmacology; some prefer jazz instead. Scientists discovered when jazz musicians improvise, their brains *turn off* areas linked to self-censoring and inhibition and *turn on* those that let self-expression flow.

In an article called "This Is Your Brain On Jazz," Charles J. Limb, MD, says, "When jazz musicians improvise, they often play with eyes closed in a distinctive, personal style that transcends traditional rules of melody and rhythm … all of a sudden, the musician is generating music that has never been heard, thought, practiced or played before. What comes out is completely spontaneous."[91]

CHARACTERISTICS OF FLOW

Maybe you don't play jazz music. You might wonder if you can still get into a flow state. If so, how would you even know? The cool thing about flow is it's ubiquitous—meaning it can be experienced by anyone, anytime, anywhere, as long as certain conditions are met. When you experience flow, eight characteristics show up:

1. Total absorption

2. Extreme focus

3. Time dilation

4. Vanishing sense of self

5. Optimal high performance

6. Shift in brain waves

7. Shortened gap to mastery

8. Release of large amounts of neurochemicals

Reviewing the list, do any feel familiar? Once I locked my RAS filter onto these eight characteristics, I started seeing them everywhere, especially in one particular scene from one particular movie.

Maybe you saw *Limitless* starring Bradley Cooper and Robert De Niro? The basic premise of the movie is how a pill can essentially unlock your brain by allowing you to use 100% of your cognitive functions. The film opens with Eddie Morra (played by Bradley Cooper) unable to complete the draft for his book. He's a huge loser with no future. All of that changes when he gets hold of a drug—NZT-48. The drug enhances his cognitive abilities.

Because the drug enables pattern recognition, increases productivity, and generates perfect mental recall, Eddie rises to the top of the financial world and attracts the attention of a tycoon named Carl Van Loon (Robert De Niro) who intends to use him to make a fortune. Not all things end well due to the drug's side effects.

In the final scene, Eddie embodies success. He maintains his wealth, publishes a book, and runs for the United States Senate. Then, Carl makes a final visit and delivers the startling news to Eddie. He has absorbed the company that produced NZT-48 and shut down Eddie's laboratory. Because Eddie's presidency is inevitable and he's apparently dependent upon NZT-48, Carl blackmails Eddie into working for him as his puppet. Eddie ignores the threat and tells Carl he's perfected the drug and weaned himself off of it, retaining his abilities without any side effects.

The climax of the movie showcases all eight flow characteristics. Although I don't want to hack you by telling you to hop over to YouTube to watch the scene, the clip might solidify the flow characteristics for you in a whole new way. If you choose to watch the three-minute scene, simply search for this term—*End of Limitless*—or keep reading the case study below.

1. Total Absorption

The final scene of the movie opens up with Eddie staring off into the distance. He isn't thinking about the past or the future—he's completely engaged in the moment. We call this the Deep Now, a space where action and awareness merge. Although he's physically immobile, his subconscious brain is on fire. He's engaged in lateral thinking, and this ultimate absorption sets up the next scene.

2. Extreme Focus

Eddie talks with Carl. He isn't distracted by Carl's threats about the future or accusations about the past. Eddie remains laser-focused on the issue at hand, refusing to work for Carl.

3. Time Dilation

In the van scene, time slows down for Eddie. He sees events unfolding seconds before they actually do. Because he's experiencing transient hypofrontality, he trades conscious processing for unconscious processing. Transient hypofrontality is a common experience with flow states. The term can be understood in three distinct parts:

- transient = *temporary*

- hypo = *the opposite of hyper*

- frontality = *the location in the brain*

Eddie's future predictions are a result of highspeed pattern recognition. He even admits this ability. "I see everything, Carl. I'm 50 moves ahead of you and everybody else."

4. Vanishing Sense of Self

Eddie continues with near-perfect decision-making. He steps toward Carl and grabs his chest, warning him about his unhealthy heart. He is confident and direct, not once doubting or judging his abnormal encounter on a busy city street.

5. Optimal High Performance

Eddie ends his exchange with Carl by telling him to vote. He then shifts his attention from this heated interaction by replying to his friend. In seamless fashion, Eddie reminds him of his lunch appointment and then walks into a Chinese restaurant.

Most people's productivity would have been sabotaged by this emotional confrontation with Carl. But Eddie? He keeps on producing, even giving his date a sincere apology for being late.

6. Shift in Brain Waves

Eddie exhibits the classic signs of all four phases of the flow cycle, each defined by unique brain waves:

- *Struggle phase*: Eddie hears about his impending confrontation with Carl. (Beta Waves)

- *Release phase*: He daydreams, taking his mind off of the matter at hand. (Alpha Waves)

- *Flow phase*: He demonstrates his superhuman ability for lateral thinking and pattern recognition. (Theta/Gamma Waves)

- *Recovery phase*: He sits down to a fantastic Chinese lunch. (Delta Waves)

7. Shortened Gap to Mastery

Eddie shocks his date with an instant mastery of a foreign language. He orders lobster and even knows enough of the culture to make a joke the waiter finds humorous.

8. Release of Large Amounts of Neurochemicals

This entire clip couldn't have been possible without a cascade of neurochemicals. Although none of the neurochemicals are named, we observe their effects.

SCIENCE FACT

For those ignorant of flow, it's easy to dismiss Hollywood films as science fiction. After all, in *Limitless*, Eddie experienced all these characteristics because of a fictitious drug called NZT-48.

The movie premise promotes the myth that we only use 10% of our brain. Supposedly, the NZT drug unlocks the other 90%, and presto—Eddie is limitless. He seduces women, completes his novel in record time, excels at the stock market, and achieves a wide array of superhuman feats.

Of course, the film has drawbacks. It's irresponsible to portray flow as the result of swallowing a pill. Sadly, many drug manufacturers have cashed in on the premise.

If you search for NZT-48 online, you'll see marketers, not scientists. The promise on their home pages is simple:

1. Wake up

2. Take a pill

3. Succeed

Their "Customer Love Team" will even rush you your order of ten free capsules, also referred to as "smart pills."

Despite all these shortcomings, *Limitless* and many other Hollywood films borrow some of their flow benefits from scientific fact.

The Hungarian psychologist Mihály Csíkszentmihályi is credited with identifying and naming the psychological concept of flow. He's the author of over 120 articles and many books, including the bestselling book *Flow: The Psychology of Optimal Experience*. In an interview with *Wired* magazine, he described flow:

> [Flow is] being completely involved in an activity for its own sake. The ego falls away. Time flies. Every action, movement, and thought follows inevitably from the previous one, like playing jazz. Your whole being is involved, and you're using your skills to the utmost.[92]

THE CAPTAIN OF FLOW

Sometimes, flow shows up in the most remarkable places. In his book *Highest Duty*, Captain Chesley "Sully" Sullenberger explains that the Canada geese with six-foot wingspans, weighing eight to eighteen pounds each, sounded like large hail pelting the plane. Moments later, he felt what every pilot fears—double engine failure resulting from a brutal bird strike.

Routine had suddenly been blown to pieces—along with the birds. The plane lost thrust and, given its low speed and low altitude over New York City—one of the most densely populated areas on the planet—Captain Sully knew he sat front and center in a seriously challenging situation.

Despite the fact that he had never requested this experience, in that instant, life sought his response. And 154 people prayed that Captain Sully's response would prove to be the right one.

Although you're probably familiar with what happened next, you may have never considered that flow showed up in the cockpit on that cold January day.

Some dismiss January 15, 2009, as a fluke or an example of luck in its purest form. Many prefer to label the whole experience as a miracle. And that's exactly what they did, referring to this event as the "Miracle on the Hudson."

But it wasn't a miracle.

For the record, I do believe in miracles. I've read about them and have even experienced a few, but I also believe in the flow that Captain Sully experienced. Because of it, he achieved what has been called the most successful ditching in aviation history.

Was he a hero?

You bet—and the rest of the crew with him. They rightfully received the highest award in aviation. But this miracle wasn't simply happenstance. Rather, by taking a closer look, it's easy to see all eight flow characteristics show up in his successful emergency landing on the Hudson River.

Captain Sully summarized his experience with flow in his interview with *CBS News* anchor Katie Couric: "For 42 years, I've been making small regular deposits in this bank of experience: education and training. And on January 15, the balance was sufficient so that I could make a very large withdrawal."[93]

CLOSE YOUR GAP DAY 20: OPTIMIZE YOUR PERFORMANCE

Although today's mission is incredibly simple, the result could be incredibly profound. By reflecting upon the lesson, you'll recall Eddie and Sully. In both cases, these men experienced optimized performance thanks to flow. But did you catch the common denominator preceding their flow? If you missed it, I'll give you a hint. It's something we don't usually enjoy.

Struggle!

On Day 22, we'll unpack the four phases of the flow cycle more in-depth:

Struggle ➡ Release ➡ Flow ➡ Recovery

For now, I want you to optimize your performance by shifting your perspective of struggle. Consider this truth:

Without pain, there is no payoff.
Without struggle, there is no Boon.

On that note, list five reasons why you're thankful for your current struggle. If you see struggle as your enemy, you'll only focus on your struggle. But if you see your struggle as a pre-loading phase to get you into flow, you'll focus on your Boon.

Five reasons I'm thankful for my struggle:

1.

2.

3.

4.

5.

DAY 21

SELF:

Silence Your Critics

You must strive to find your own voice. Because the longer you
wait to begin, the less likely you are to find it at all.

—John Keating, *Dead Poets Society*

How many of these statements have you thought about yourself?

1. I often get in my own way.

2. I'm my own worst enemy.

3. I'm self-critical.

4. I struggle with self-limiting beliefs.

5. I doubt my own abilities.

6. I don't see my own greatness.

7. I know all my weaknesses.

8. It's tough for me to identify my strengths.

9. I never finish anything.

10. I don't want to put something out unless it's perfect.

If you're like most people, you've let one or more of these statements hack you. This unhealthy and unproductive cycle is a Hack Attack. In Days 3 and 4, we discovered we're each the biggest culprit in our own lives. That's the problem, but let's discover the solution. How do we get out of our own way? A scene from *Dead Poets Society* offers clarity.[94]

You might wonder, *Why so many movie references?* In my coaching, speaking, and writing, I often reference films to illustrate truths. Since movies are modern-day stories, they open us up in a unique way. I trust this one will too.

UNPACK A HACK

In *Dead Poets Society*, Todd Anderson (played by Ethan Hawke) exhibited classic signs of someone who has been hacked. We'll unpack his hack one phrase at a time. In the process, we'll also unpack how Mr. John Keating (played by Robin Williams) snapped him out of the hack and helped him get into a flow state. This case study will also give us clarity for overcoming our own hacks and experiencing flow.

> *Mr. Keating*: Mr. Anderson, I see you sitting there in agony. Come on, Todd, step up. Let's put you out of your misery.

Don't be fooled. Flow can happen to anyone at any time as long as certain conditions are met. It's not just reserved for athletes or daredevils. Activities like speaking, writing, arts, business, or any other activity can induce flow. To get into flow, we must be challenged, and that's exactly what Todd experienced in Mr. Keating's invitation to stand up in front of his peers and recite a poem.

> *Todd:* I didn't do it. I didn't write a poem.

Like many of us, Todd resisted struggle. Rather than getting in the game and possibly making a fool of himself, Todd settled for sitting on the bench. But as long as we keep running from a chance at failing, we also run from a chance at flow. Remember, flow requires struggle as a preloading phase.

> *Mr. Keating:* Mr. Anderson thinks that everything inside of him is worthless and embarrassing. Isn't that right, Todd? Isn't that your worst fear? Well, I think you're wrong. I think you have something inside of you that is worth a great deal.

> [Mr. Keating walks up to the blackboard and begins to write.]

Mr. Keating knew a lecture wouldn't help unhack his student. To experience flow, Todd would need a large dose of unpredictability, something we call a flow trigger. (We'll discover nine common flow triggers on Day 25.)

> *Mr. Keating:* "I sound my barbaric yawp over the rooftops of the world." W. W. Uncle Walt again. Now, for those of you who don't know, a yawp is a loud cry or yell. Now, Todd, I would like you to give us a demonstration of a barbaric yawp. Come on. You can't yawp sitting down. Let's go. Come on. Up.

> [Todd reluctantly stands and follows Mr. Keating to the front.]

Although Mr. Keating wanted to stretch Todd, he wasn't trying to snap him. Too little challenge, and Todd will shut off because he's bored. Too much challenge, and Todd will shut down because he's anxious.

Mr. Keating: You gotta get in yawping stance.

Mr. Keating continued to push Todd by introducing a clear goal. He wanted Todd to perform a poem in real time.

Todd: A yawp?

Mr. Keating: No, not just a yawp. A barbaric yawp.

Todd (quietly): Yawp.

Mr. Keating: Come on, louder.

Todd (quietly): Yawp.

Mr. Keating: No, that's a mouse. Come on. Louder.

Todd: Yawp.

Mr. Keating: Oh, good God, boy. Yell like a man!

Todd (shouting): Yawp!

Mr. Keating: There it is. You see, you have a barbarian in you, after all.

[Todd goes to return to his seat, but Mr. Keating stops him.]

Mr. Keating gave Todd feedback loops. After three underwhelming yawps, finally, he let Todd move on with his poem.

Mr. Keating: Now, you don't get away that easy.

[Mr. Keating turns Todd around and points out a picture on the wall.]

Mr. Keating: The picture of Uncle Walt up there. What does he remind you of? Don't think. Answer. Go on.

[Mr. Keating begins to circle around Todd.]

Todd: A m-m-madman.

Mr. Keating: What kind of madman? Don't think about it. Just answer again.

Todd: A c-crazy madman.

Mr. Keating: No, you can do better than that. Free up your mind. Use your imagination. Say the first thing that pops into your head, even if it's total gibberish. Go on, go on.

Notice the instructions Mr. Keating gave. *"Free up your mind. Use your imagination. Say the first thing that pops into your head, even if it's total gibberish."* All these prompts were designed to help Todd silence his inner critic.

Todd: Uh, uh, a sweaty-toothed madman.

Mr. Keating: Good God, boy, there's a poet in you, after all. There, close your eyes. Close your eyes. Close 'em. Now, describe what you see.

[Mr. Keating puts his hands over Todd's eyes, and they both begin to spin around slowly.]

Mr. Keating utilized Flawless Idea Anatomy elements like promotion when he affirmed Todd in front of the other boys. He then used Focus Filters like urgency, agency, and energy. He told him three times to close his eyes. By spinning Todd and blocking his vision, he forced him to zero in on the present task.

Todd: Uh, I-I close my eyes.

Mr. Keating: Yes?

Todd: Uh, and this image floats beside me.

Mr. Keating: A sweaty-toothed madman?

Todd: A sweaty-toothed madman with a stare that pounds my brain.

Mr. Keating: Oh, that's excellent. Now, give him action. Make him do something.

Todd: H-His hands reach out and choke me.

Mr. Keating: That's it. Wonderful. Wonderful.

[Mr. Keating removes his hands from Todd, but Todd keeps his eyes closed.]

Mr. Keating provided more feedback loops.

Todd: And-and all the time he's mumbling.

Mr. Keating: What's he mumbling?

Todd: M-Mumbling, "Truth. Truth is like, like a blanket that always leaves your feet cold."

[The students begin to laugh, and Todd opens his eyes. Mr. Keating quickly gestures for him to close them again.]

The laughs from fellow students almost hacked Todd out of flow. Thankfully, Mr. Keating recognized it and covered his eyes again. This focusing technique enabled him to maintain flow and silence his inner critic.

> *Mr. Keating*: Forget them, forget them. Stay with the blanket. Tell me about that blanket.

Mr. Keating observed Todd's pattern recognition and lateral thinking. He invited Todd to keep making connections.

> *Todd*: Y-Y-Y-You push it, stretch it, it'll never be enough. You kick at it, beat it—it'll never cover any of us. From the moment we enter crying to the moment we leave dying, it will just cover your face as you wail and cry and scream.

> [Todd opens his eyes. The class is silent. Then, they begin to clap and cheer.]

> *Mr. Keating* (whispering to Todd): Don't you forget this.

Both Todd and Mr. Keating witness the neurochemicals that supported this flow state. Todd clearly reached a new level. He shortened his path to mastery, tasted optimal human performance, and felt the effects of an inner critic finally bound and gagged. His class cheered for a peer who did his best, felt his best, and achieved a new level of productivity.

FACTS BEHIND FLOW

At first glance, you might chalk this up as a mere story. But those who know about flow know better. Once you've been exposed to flow, you're more aware of it in your life and in the lives of others. You know that popular explanations like "natural talent," "gifted prodigy," and even the "Miracle on the Hudson" are incomplete at best.

Brace yourself—we're only getting started. Once I learned how to silence my inner critic, the rules of the game changed forever.

As I mentioned earlier, I was hacked so badly that I became addicted to self-injury. My inner critic accused me night and day. As a young adult, I found relief through a blade I took to my body. This temporary escape only led me further into darkness. Thankfully, God rescued me from this self-destructive prison. Today, I maintain Unhackability in work and life.

In nearly two decades of freedom, I've met plenty of stuck souls. Although I may have self-injured with a knife, many other people are in a prison just as dark. Their self-limiting beliefs hack them night and day, and they self-injure through a variety of other mediums.

Wherever you are in your journey, it's time to embody more levels of freedom by experiencing deeper levels of flow. For today's mission, please start by reading Todd's poem.

I close my eyes, and this image floats beside me.
A sweaty-toothed mad man with a stare that pounds my brain.
His hands reach out and choke me, and all the time he's mumbling.
"Truth, truth."
Like a blanket that always leaves your feet cold.
You push it, stretch it, but it'll never be enough.
You kick at it, beat it, it'll never cover any of us.
From the moment we enter crying,
to the moment we leave dying,
it'll just cover your face
as you wail and cry and scream.

CLOSE YOUR GAP DAY 21: SILENCE YOUR CRITICS

Now, it's time to write your own Boon Poem. As you begin, remember Mr. Keating's advice to all of us who have hacked ourselves with self-limiting beliefs:

> Well, I think you're wrong. I think you have something inside you that is worth a great deal.

Boon Poem Instructions:

This exercise isn't one where you use your conscious mind. Rather, shut down your prefrontal cortex. Don't try to make sense and don't aim for perfection. Instead, put your pen to paper or your fingers on the keyboard. The trick is to keep on writing or typing.

The topic of your poem is your Boon. Write how you feel about your Boon at this point in time.

My Boon Poem

I close my eyes, and this image floats beside me …

DAY 22

CYCLE:
Unpack Your Cycle

If we are hunting the highest version of ourselves, then we need to turn work into play and not the other way round.

—Steven Kotler

I n Spring 2016, my friend David and I flew from Ohio to Florida. Although we both enjoy personal growth and business development, we had never attended such a conference together. I always went to mine, and he always went to his. This time was different. We were going to learn and grow together—at least, that was the plan.

On the flight to Palm Beach, we sat near each other and mapped out several gaps in the business, including products we still needed to create. I opened my laptop and typed notes. We knew what we needed to do, but we could never find the time. Since we each had a family of five, it seemed as though life kept getting in the way, preventing us from filming these five critical courses:

1. A free seven-day book course leading to Author Academy Elite (MyBookHook.com)

2. A smaller paid program for those who weren't ready to do Author Academy Elite (MyBookBlueprint. com)

3. A free seven-day course leading to the Your Secret Name 5-Week Journey

4. A free seven-day course leading to The Deeper Path Cohort

5. A free seven-day course leading to Dream Job Bootcamp

We checked into our hotel and then headed over to the conference venue. Although the vibe was much different than I expected for a professional conference, I maintained an open mind. I kept a positive attitude throughout the entire registration process. The opening session finally began.

After an hour of bass pumping, awkward breaks for random dancing, crude jokes from the stage, excessive vulgar language from the speaker, and a woman next to us dancing in a sports bra, I had enough. In the context of *Unhackable* (Day 14: Agency—Choose Your Inputs), the conference clearly didn't match my Boon. Sure, there could have been a nugget of wisdom here or there, but I was too distracted by the space to absorb anything. Nevertheless, I tried to stick it out a few hours longer.

After our dinner break, I threw in the towel and headed back to our hotel room to work on my Boon. *Elixir Project* was still unfinished, and I wasn't about to be hacked again.

That next day, David wanted to give the conference another chance. He headed out for the venue while I stayed in the hotel room and wrote. With my Boon deadline set and the penalty signed via the contract with my editor (Day 13—Urgency:

Establish Your Deadline), I knew I needed to make some serious progress. That day, I cranked out a number of chapters in the book.

After dinner, David returned to the room with a dejected look on his face. "I'm not growing! I can't do this anymore," he exclaimed.

I closed my laptop and looked out the window. My mind drifted. We had invested time and money in the flight, the hotel, and the days away from the business. Our plans were clearly hacked.

Gazing out the glass, I spotted a tall parking garage a couple of buildings down overlooking the water and palm trees off in the distance. A new idea started forming. We could film those five courses right on top of the parking garage! Although we didn't have the proper equipment, we each had our smartphones. We lacked our usual props—lights, microphones, and scripts, but we had something even better: sunlight, time, and scenery. Now in a new city without all the distractions of home, maybe this was our perfect opportunity to experience flow.

I sold David on the idea, and we clarified Our three Focus Filters

1. *Urgency* = We established a deadline. We knew our plane would leave in a few days, and we had forty videos in front of us.

2. *Agency* = We chose our inputs. Rather than sitting in a conference that wasn't a match, we created a new space conducive to our immediate goal.

3. *Energy* = We reallocated our attention, stayed on task, and kept the goal front and center. In our downtime back at the hotel, we hired freelancers to create logos for the five products we were making.

THE FOUR STAGES OF FLOW

On top of that parking garage, during those four days in March 2016, I experienced all four stages of the flow cycle over and over again. Before I tell you *how* I experienced the stages, I'll first share what each stage looks and feels like. As you read the description, reflect on your own life and determine if you've ever experienced a flow cycle.

According to Herb Benson, MD, from Harvard, there are four stages in a flow cycle:

1. Struggle = Beta Brain Waves

You need to encounter a certain level of stress to get into flow. This is a preloading phase. Maybe you're facing a deadline, a problem, or some other kind of dilemma. Your body and brain need to feel a challenge with stakes for winning and losing.

> Stress is a physiological response to any change. … Good stress, also called "eustress," gives us energy and motivates us to strive and produce. We see eustress in elite athletes, creative artists, and all kinds of high achievers. Anyone who's clinched an important deal or had a good performance review, for example, enjoys the benefits of eustress, such as clear thinking, focus, and creative insight.[95]

2. Release = Alpha Brain Waves

Focusing on the problem is often the worst thing you can do. Remember, your conscious mind processes between forty– 200 bits of information per second. This is incredibly slow. However, your subconscious mind processes billions of bits of information per second.

By taking your mind off the matter at hand, you get out of your own way. Your RAS filter kicks into overdrive and prepares to solve the problem for you. The seeds of many breakthroughs are sown within this phase.

3. Flow = Theta and Gamma Brain Waves

We've seen this stage in Sully's emergency landing on the Hudson River in Day 20 and Todd's poem from *Dead Poets Society* in Day 21. This is where you feel your best and perform your best. You experience lateral thinking, pattern recognition, and near-perfect decision-making. You're 500% more productive, and you may achieve a gamma spike similar to a eureka moment.

4. Recovery = Delta Brain Waves

This is the phase most high performers try to skip. Going from superhuman back to super normal is hard. As a result, many athletes over-train and suffer negative results over time. You were designed with recovery in mind. This stage includes proper food, hydration, sleep, and sunlight.

CONNECTING THE DOTS ON THE ROOFTOP

Once you understand these four flow stages, it's much easier to spot them in your life. This is the power of the RAS—your mind's eye. Looking back, I realize David and I created conditions favorable for flow:

1. Struggle = Beta Brain Waves

On the plane ride over, David and I identified the challenges in the business. We knew what we needed to do, we just didn't have the time or space to do it.

Additional Example: I often take on challenges in line with my Boon that will intentionally stretch me. Too little stretch, and

I'm bored. Too much stretch, and I snap. I often rely on the deadline. It's the jumpstart I need to experience flow.

2. Release = Alpha Brain Waves

David went back to the conference. I started cranking on the *Elixir Project* manuscript after I did an intense workout that morning. I took my mind off of the challenges David and I had discussed by jogging along the beach.

Additional Example: My biggest breakthroughs happen during my workouts or shortly after when I'm showering. I never step into the shower or a workout trying to solve a problem. I let my subconscious go and often experience enhanced creativity.

3. Flow = Theta and Gamma Brain Waves

David and I produced over forty videos in a few days. We broke up each large group of videos with a mile walk to the smoothie shop. This took my mind off of the next group of videos. We engaged in exercise, conversation, and hydration.

Additional Example: When writing or creating, sometimes I'll listen to the same song on repeat thirty or sixty times in a row. Or I listen to an extended playlist. I usually prefer songs without lyrics, though not all the time, and I am never interrupted by ads.

4. Recovery = Delta Brain Waves

By far, this is the phase I struggle with the most. After filming for four days, David demanded we go on a long walk to The Breakers, a luxury Palm Beach Resort. We enjoyed an amazing lunch with an incredible view of the ocean. This meal capped off our flow cycle.

Additional Example: I enjoy recovery once I'm in it, but earlier in my career, this was the one stage I tried to skip. In my mind, it felt unproductive. It took me a while to realize I was only cheating myself, my productivity, and my chances to experience more flow. Now I enjoy much more flow because I've integrated recovery into my daily schedule.

CLOSE YOUR GAP DAY 22: UNPACK YOUR CYCLE

Think back to a time you felt flow. Remember, flow is a spectrum. You may have experienced micro flow or macro flow. The size or length is irrelevant. I want you to increase your awareness around flow—*when* you experience it and *how* you experience it.

Free write your experience with each stage. Free writing means letting your mind go and putting your thoughts on your page without judging.

1. **Struggle:** Describe a time when you felt what Dr. Herb Benson refers to as *eustress*—the good stress.

2. **Release:** What do you do to take your mind off the problem? This isn't about distracting yourself with media—it's about letting yourself go.

3. **Flow:** Describe a time when you were in flow—the optimal state of human performance where you do your best and feel your best.

4. **Recovery:** What do you do to rest and build yourself back up again?

DAY 23

MASTERY:
Embody Your Mastery

*My dad encouraged us to fail. Growing up, he would ask us
what we failed at that week. If we didn't have something, he
would be disappointed. It changed my mindset at an early age
that failure is not the outcome, failure is not trying.*

—Sara Blakely

Your brain stops developing after the first few years
of life.

That's what scientists *used* to think. Thankfully,
recent research on neuroplasticity disproves this:

Neuroplasticity is an umbrella term referring to the ability of your brain to reorganize itself, both physically and
functionally, throughout your life due to your environment, behavior, thinking, and emotions. The concept
of neuroplasticity is not new and mentions of a mal-
leable brain go all the way back to the 1800s, but with
the relatively recent capability to visually "see" into the
brain allowed by functional magnetic resonance imaging

(fMRI), science has confirmed this incredible morphing ability of the brain beyond a doubt.[96]

When we learn something or engage in new experiences, our neural circuits alter our brain. Neurons communicate with each other through special junctions called synapses. Repeated exposure causes these specific circuits to fire again and again, and the stronger these synaptic connections become, the more our brain is rewired.

Neuroplasticity is neutral, meaning it can work for us or against us. And it can create conditions for slavery or mastery, depending on the context. Notice the difference:

1. ADDICTIONS ➡ SLAVERY

Addicts have different brain scans than people without addictions. A new study has found that the brains of people addicted to pornography behave in a similar way to those of alcoholics or drug addicts.[97]

Academics from Cambridge University studied people who said they had a problem with the amount of pornography they use. Scientists found that part of their brains "lit up" when shown explicit material—the same activity that is reported in the brains of other types of addicts.

Addictions of all kinds rewire our brains. They alter our neurochemistry and hack us by preventing flow. Obviously, this is the negative side of neuroplasticity. However, there's good news. Neuroplasticity can rewire our brains positively too.

2. FLOW STATES ➡ MASTERY

In several popular scenes from *The Matrix*, Neo (played by Keanu Reeves) experiences something now known as automatic learning. Through a computer program downloaded into his brain via electrodes, Neo becomes an instant expert in martial arts and other skill-based activities.

Although *The Matrix* is fictional, flow isn't. And thanks to flow, we can create and strengthen new neural pathways. Neuroplasticity enables us to shorten the gap to mastery. Tomorrow, we'll explore how this has helped surfers, snowboarders, and gymnasts. Today, let's look at how it helped out the military.

When DARPA researchers induced flow artificially (using transcranial stimulation), they found that the target acquisition skills of military snipers improved 230%. In a similar (but nonmilitary) study, researchers at Advanced Brain Monitoring in Carlsbad, CA, found that an artificially induced flow state cut the time it took to train novice snipers up to the expert level by 50%.[98]

This sounds intriguing. However, not many of us are becoming snipers, nor do we have access to transcranial stimulation. So, what about the rest of us who want to shorten the gap to mastery? What's our solution?

NEUROPLASTICITY FOR THE MASSES

The truth is everyone can benefit from neuroplasticity. Here's only one example in the field of leadership development. Conventional wisdom suggests leaders are born, not built. Yet a growing field called "neuroleadership" aims to change this stereotype by applying brain training techniques originally designed to help make better soldiers. Neuroleadership helps less-gifted business leaders become better and good leaders become great ones. Neuroplasticity makes this possible. If it didn't, we'd be all be locked into one job, unable to gain new mastery.

We're all beneficiaries of neuroplasticity. Without it, I'd still be a pastor. Do a quick Google search, and you'll discover I don't have a business or marketing degree. In fact, I never took either of these classes. I excelled in Greek and Hebrew, not economics and branding. I earned a Master of Divinity degree, not a Master of Business Administration—a Doctor of Ministry degree, not a doctorate in marketing.

Despite having zero business experience, I not only went on to learn these other disciplines, but I also mastered them in a short amount of time. A couple of years later, I wrote a business book and was invited to speak at business conferences alongside legends like Brian Tracy.

I did this through flow and shortening the gap to mastery. This was true with becoming a fiction writer as well. After twelve years of writing, I wasn't supposed to cross over from nonfiction to fiction, but I did. These two examples aren't unique to me.

Remember, flow is ubiquitous. Anyone can experience it anywhere, providing certain conditions are met. We can all shorten the gap to mastery by experiencing flow and enjoying the benefits of positive neuroplasticity.

CLOSE YOUR GAP DAY 23: EMBODY YOUR MASTERY

It's time for you to Embody Your Mastery. What skills would you like to add to your arsenal? Make a list. What abilities would push you closer to your Boon? Take inventory. In my experience, the *what* question was always more difficult than the *how* question.

I ended up pursuing mastery of business, marketing, and fiction by utilizing Deliberate Magnetic Focus and Optimal Human Performance—focus and flow. Begin the process by first evaluating your current quality of neuroplasticity.

1. Have you created conditions for slavery (addictions)?

2. Be honest. Are you addicted to anything (substances, activities, etc.)? If so, what are these addictions?

3. Did you leave any out? Go back to #2 and write them out.

4. Do you understand that these addictions are hacking you and preventing you from reaching greater levels of flow?

5. Do you want to experience the positive side of neuroplasticity and rewire your brain to achieve your Boon?

6. What new skills or abilities would you like to master?

7. From your list above, pick the #1 skill or ability you need next.

In the remainder of the flow module, we'll help you shorten the gap to mastery through Optimal Human Performance—specifically the nine flow triggers in Day 24. Your Boon could be closer than you think.

DAY 24

NEUROCHEMICALS:
Engage Your Neurochemicals

Americans are literally killing themselves trying to achieve artificially the same sensations that flow produces naturally.

—Steven Kotler

You can either experience the benefits of flow the way biology intended or settle for an inferior substitute.

Norepinephrine, dopamine, endorphins, anandamide, and serotonin are endogenous, meaning they originate within you naturally. These neurochemicals result from a flow state and come with zero drawbacks. In fact, when in a flow state, you experience a concentrated "cocktail" of neurochemicals without the negative side effects.

Popular drugs many people use are an irresponsible attempt to mimic a flow-like experience with much less effectiveness. Besides lower concentrations of neurochemicals, each artificial flow substitute carries serious consequences with it. Notice how each drug attempts to replicate the neurochemical's benefit:

AUTHENTIC	ARTIFICIAL	BENEFIT
NOREPINEPHRINE	Speed	increases heart rate, emotional control, attention
DOPAMINE	Cocaine	superhuman focus, pattern recognition, skill-enhacing abilities
ENDORPHINS	Heroin Oxycontin	withstand discomfort
ANANDAMIDE	Marijuana	augments lateral thinking, link contrasting ideas together
SEROTONIN	Antidepressants	stay on task in spite of pain

In his book *The Rise of Superman*, Steven Kotler provides additional commentary on the recent surge of drug usage related to the topic of flow:

> In America, over 22 percent of the population has an illicit drug problem; one out of ten take antidepressants; 26 percent of kids are on stimulants. ... And prescription drugs? They've just surpassed car accidents as the number one cause of accidental death. Add this up and you'll find a trillion-dollar public-health crisis. ... In other words, Americans are literally killing themselves to achieve artificially the same sensations that flow produces naturally. Of course, as a perfect endogenous combination of these drugs, flow is also a major rush. But unlike the dead-end highs currently plaguing public health, flow doesn't sidetrack one's life; it revitalizes it. Flow is the rush of possibility. As Devore concludes: "I really think we're the next stage in human evolution."

Although I agree with Kotler, I would tweak Devore's evolution statement. We've always had the capacity for flow, but the truth is we're only beginning to peel back the layers. We're learning how to maximize these neurochemicals and leverage them to our advantage in work and play.

If you have any doubts, look no further than sports. The Olympic games of today compared to those of previous generations look dramatically different. MTV News made it easy to spot the differences in a one-minute video posted on YouTube that compares the 1950s Olympics to the 2016 games side-by-side. If you watch the video *"Gymnastics Have Changed for the Better | Rio Olympics | MTV News,"* you might think you're watching two different species competing.[99]

Trends like this aren't isolated to the Olympics. If you track the progress of any sport, you'll notice dramatic shifts. Surfing is over one thousand years old. Twenty-five years ago, the biggest wave ever ridden was twenty-five feet. Today, the record tops over eighty feet tall.[100] Snowboarding has experienced a similar shift. In 1992, the largest gap ever cleared was forty feet. Today, that record has more than quadrupled to 187 feet.

Either we're physically evolving in real time or we're upgrading neurobiologically. Obviously, the neurochemicals released in flow are the catalyst for this change.

STEP TOWARD THE STRUGGLE

Modern conveniences and soft mindsets choke out flow for most people. As NCAA Head Coach Tom Ryan warns, "Life in the twenty-first century is designed for comfort—just look around. We have upgrades for everything—airfare, tickets to the big game, and even our phones. But what's the real cost of comfort?"[101]

The answer to Ryan's question is simple. The cost of comfort is neurochemicals. Without struggle, there is no flow.

In my life, I've come to peace with this truth: If I want the chemicals, I need the challenge. Extreme adventurer Mike Horn agrees. "The moment it becomes a little too difficult we step away, and that's just the moment that I like to step into it."[102]

Think about your Boon for a moment. Imagine if you were able to utilize these flow benefits while pursuing your Boon. Would they help you achieve it?

- Increased heart rate, emotional control, attention

- Superhuman focus, pattern recognition, skill-enhancing abilities

- Augmented lateral thinking

- Power to link contrasting ideas together

- Ability to withstand discomfort and stay on task in spite of pain

Maybe these five neurochemicals are heaven's gift to help you achieve your Boon.

CLOSE YOUR GAP DAY 24: ENGAGE YOUR NEUROCHEMICALS

Instead of talking about flow, what if you experienced flow—like right now? Flow isn't a spectator sport. You need to feel it for yourself. If you're ready to jump into a micro flow state, then please follow these six steps:

1. Turn off all distractions. (This means all dings, beeps, buzzes—everything.)

2. Get a pair of headphones and turn the sound up.

3. Prepare to be completely focused for five minutes.

4. Go to YouTube and play this video on full screen—
   "Sleeping At Last - 'Saturn' (Official Music Video)."[103]

5. Do nothing but watch the video.

6. Choose to let your mind go as you watch the video
   and listen to the music.

After the song is done, write whatever comes to your mind
in the space below. If you need silence, write in silence. If
you'd like to hear this song again while you write, then play
it again. If you need a longer version, purchase it, download
it, and put it on repeat.

My Micro Flow Session

DAY 25

TRIGGERS:
Understand Your Triggers

*A happy man is too satisfied with the present
to dwell too much on the future.*

—Albert Einstein

Throughout the centuries, warriors attributed super-human success on the battlefield to a gift from the gods. Writers credited breakthroughs in their books to visits from their muse. Because we didn't understand flow until the last couple of decades, we didn't know how to produce it on demand.

Today, thanks to advances in neuroscience, we're more aware of the conditions conducive to flow. As a result, Unhackable people leverage these triggers and reverse engineer the process.

Different neuroscientists call flow triggers by different names. Some only have a few on their lists while others break them down into smaller categories, making bigger lists.

I've identified five internal flow triggers and four external ones. Unpacking these triggers will help you understand them and, more importantly, organize your life around flow. (Some of these might be familiar because we've already encountered them within the Idea and Focus components.)

5 INTERNAL FLOW TRIGGERS

1. The Deep Now

Success demands singularity of time and space (no switch-tasking).

As long as you're belaboring the past or worrying about the future, flow will elude you. To experience flow, you must be fully open to the present. Experts call it the Deep Now or the Elongated Now. Bottom line, success demands singularity of time and space. Stay away from switch-tasking and dissociation. Step toward the struggle. Embrace the acute pain and live from the gift of the present.

2. Defined Deadline

Output is no longer optional.

I've said it before: Desire without a deadline is simply a pipe dream. But a deadline isn't enough. Just because you have a *destination* doesn't mean you also have a *motivation*. Urgency is what gets you moving in full force. Paying a penalty for missing your deadline injects a serious dose of motivation.

3. Authentic Ownership

Participation is mandatory, and I influence the outcome.

If you don't believe you matter, then you've already stepped out of flow. Personally, I like the pressure of participation— every single day. Pressure lets me know I have the ability to influence the outcome.

When my son first started playing basketball years ago, he was dejected after a game. I asked him why. He told me it was because no one passed him the ball. He was right. No one passed him the ball the entire game. But I knew why.

"Son, that's because you told your team you didn't want the ball.

"What do you mean, Dad?" he asked. "I didn't say one word the entire game."

"Ah, but you did," I said. "Your body language told everyone not to pass to you."

He admitted he was scared to get the ball because he didn't want to miss a shot. Without even saying a word, he gave off the frequency that he didn't want to participate, and the other players heard him loud and clear.

Since then, he's changed his body language, and the results are unbelievable. Although he's not the highest scorer on the team as of now, he's an important asset and regularly makes key plays that influence the outcome of the game.

4. Real Risk

There's a personal cost for failing.

Risk is relative. It doesn't mean doing death-defying stunts, although it could. Many surgeons feel flow on a daily basis. Todd Anderson felt flow when he stood up in front of his class and shared his poetry in the *Dead Poets Society* clip. I experience flow by writing books and leading masterminds.

The common denominator is simple: there is a cost for failing. Todd risked the ridicule of his peers. Surgeons risk the health of their patients. I risk connection with my readers and clients.

I once knew an old man who used to say, "If it don't cost much, it ain't worth much." Intuitively, your subconscious knows this is true.

5. Rich Rewards

Autotelic experiences are embedded with purpose.

Mihály Csíkszentmihályi, the author of *Flow*, described people who are internally driven as autotelic. Something that is autotelic is described as "having a purpose in, and not apart from, itself."[104]

The word comes from the Greek αὐτοτελής, autotelēs (from αὐτός, autos, "self," and τέλος, telos, "goal"). This self-determination is very different than external drive, where things such as comfort, money, power, or fame motivate.

Think back to the Olympians, Todd's poem, or even people who do BASE jumping off mountains in wingsuits. In one sense, each has an autotelic experience with flow. The rush of neurochemicals will keep the Olympians competing, Todd speaking, and wingsuit athletes flying. However, if they continue with their flow-based activities, eventually the Olympians will want gold, Todd will want applause, and the wingsuit athletes will want sponsors.

So, in another sense, each has an external goal too. I understand and agree with Csíkszentmihályi's premise; however, I think it's limiting.

Sure, experiencing flow is the internal goal, but it's also the vehicle that drives us to an equally important external goal. One without the other is meaningless, and both are dependent upon each other. The Boon Circle© illustrates this point.

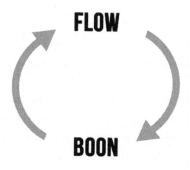

4 EXTERNAL FLOW TRIGGERS

1. Clear Goal

This is a big why combined with a big win.

Flow doesn't favor fuzziness. You know this from earlier: If you want to claim a big win, you need to clarify a big why.

JFK's goal was clear: to land a man on the moon by the end of the decade. His speech made this abundantly clear.

> For the eyes of the world now look into space, to the moon and to the planets beyond. ... I am delighted that this university is playing a part in putting a man on the moon as part of a great national effort of the United States of America. ... And this will be done in the decade of the sixties.

> Well, space is there, and we're going to climb it, and the moon and the planets are there, and new hopes for knowledge and peace are there. And, therefore, as we set sail, we ask God's blessing on the most hazardous and dangerous and greatest adventure on which man has ever embarked. [105]

But JFK also knew a clear goal wasn't enough. If he wanted a big win, he needed a big why. Again, he made this clear in his speech.

> We shall not see space filled with weapons of mass destruction, but with instruments of knowledge and understanding.

> Yet the vows of this Nation can only be fulfilled if we in this Nation are first. ... Our leadership in science and in industry, our hopes for peace and security, our obligations to ourselves as well as others, all require us to make this

effort, to solve these mysteries, to solve them for the good of all men, and to become the world's leading space-faring nation.

We set sail on this new sea because there is new knowledge to be gained, and new rights to be won, and they must be won and used for the progress of all people. For space science, like nuclear science and all technology, has no conscience of its own. Whether it will become a force for good or ill depends on man, and only if the United States occupies a position of pre-eminence can we help decide whether this new ocean will be a sea of peace or a new terrifying theater of war.

JFK's big why fueled a big win, evidenced by the team of 400,000 people securing victory in the Space Race. These men and women often experienced flow states that helped them achieve the impossible.

2. Unpredictability

Neuroplasticity is the byproduct of new pathways.

As we've studied, when you learn something new or engage in unfamiliar experiences, your neural circuits alter your brain. Neurons communicate with one another through special junctions called synapses. Repeated exposure causes these specific circuits to fire again and again. The stronger these synaptic connections become, the more your brain is rewired.

Neurons that fire together, wire together.

Neuroplasticity is neutral, meaning it can work for you or against you. It can create conditions for slavery or mastery, depending on the context. Thanks to flow, you can create and strengthen new neural pathways. This neuroplasticity enables you to shorten the gap to mastery.

3. Feedback Loops

Truth-tellers fast-track flow.

In some ways, flow is a team effort. Of course, you're the sole benefactor of the neurochemicals racing through your brain. However, to experience and sustain flow, you often need feedback loops that provide data and allow you to course-correct.

Todd had Mr. Keating. Olympians have coaches. I had Julie, my editor.

4. Challenge to Competence Ratio

A perfect blend means I'll be perfectly present.

"The toughest athlete in the world is a 62-year-old woman." This description, spoken in 2011, sounded accurate. Who else in their right mind would attempt to swim 110 miles from Cuba to Florida? As could be expected, endurance swimmer Diana Nyad fell short of her goal. With this fourth failed attempt, most people would have quit forever. Not Nyad.

She first tried in 1978, nearly half a life earlier. At that time, she swam inside a 20×40-foot steel shark cage for nearly forty-two hours. Strong westerly winds and eight-foot swells slammed against the cage. Although she made it seventy-six miles, her course proved anything but straight. She lost twenty-nine pounds in less than two days of swimming before doctors made her stop.

According to *New York Daily News*, "the elusive dream receded from the forefront of her mind but it never disappeared entirely. When Nyad turned 60, she started thinking about her limited time on this planet and could not forgive herself for the time she already wasted on negative thoughts. ... She vowed, in her 60s, to conquer the seemingly insurmountable journey she failed to finish in her 20s."[106]

In 2013, Nyad tried it again for the fifth time. She had every reason to quit while attempting the 110-mile swim from Cuba to Florida—this time without a shark cage. After nearly fifty-three hours of swimming, on September 3, 2013, at the age of sixty-four, she achieved her ultimate Boon.[107]

Notice the chart below. It's all about perception. On the left side, you'll see perceived challenges. If the challenge is high and your skills are too low, then you feel anxious. But if your skills are high and the challenge is too low, you're bored.

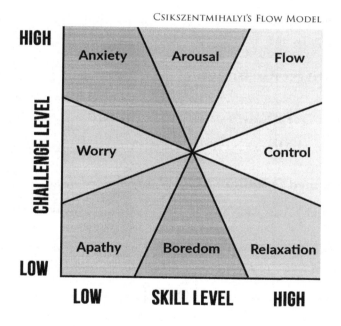

CSIKSZENTMIHALYI'S FLOW MODEL

You want what's called the flow channel. This is the perfect blend of stretch without snap. This is what Diana Nyad experienced. She had been there before—four other times. Each time, she bumped up against a skills deficit.

Although she got into flow, the challenge was too difficult, and she had to stop. On the fifth and final swim, her skills improved enough to keep her in flow and achieve her Boon.

CLOSE YOUR GAP DAY 25: UNDERSTAND YOUR TRIGGERS

You've explored the five internal triggers and four external triggers. It's time to evaluate yourself. How much of your life is organized around flow? Please answer the questions below or take the *free* online version, which will automatically calculate your score and send you a report. Simply visit UnhackableBook.com.

For each question, circle the response that closest reflects your experience.

Flow Trigger Assessment:

1. **The Deep Now:** *I only focus on one task at a time.*

   Never | Almost Never | Often | Almost Always | Always

2. **Defined Deadline:** *I have clearly defined deadlines.*

   Never | Almost Never | Often | Almost Always | Always

3. **Authentic Ownership:** *My life requires me to show up filled up, and I know I influence the outcome.*

   Never | Almost Never | Often | Almost Always | Always

4. **Real Risk:** *With my commitments, I have a real personal cost for failing.*

   Never | Almost Never | Often | Almost Always | Always

5. **Rich Rewards:** *I experience flow states that are integrated with Boon achievement.*

   Never | Almost Never | Often | Almost Always | Always

6. **Clear Goal:** *I have a big why combined with a big win.*

   Never | Almost Never | Often | Almost Always | Always

7. **Unpredictability:** *My brain experiences large amounts of neuroplasticity.*

   Never | Almost Never | Often | Almost Always | Always

8. **Feedback Loops:** *I have truth-tellers and data to help me fast-track flow.*

   Never | Almost Never | Often | Almost Always | Always

9. **Challenge to Competence Ratio:** *My life is a perfect blend of high challenge and high skills.*

   Never | Almost Never | Often | Almost Always | Always

Flow Trigger Scoring

1. Of your nine questions above, please count up how many fit each of the five categories and write that number in the respective blank below:

   Never: _____ x (1) =
   Almost Never: _____ x (2) =
   Often: _____ x (3) =
   Almost Always: _____ x (4) =
   Always: _____ x (5) =

   TOTAL: _____

2. Multiply each number you wrote in each blank by the number to the right in parentheses.

Flow Trigger Key

Page#: Total all five numbers from the evaluation above and reference the Flow Trigger Key below.

- 1–9: My life contains little to no flow. I am under-performing. I rarely accomplish things, and I don't feel satisfied.

- 10–18: I have experienced flow a few times. When I did, I felt great, but my life doesn't contain enough triggers to reproduce it on a regular basis.

- 19–27: I experience flow sometimes. My life contains some of the required triggers to help me get into flow. I feel great about 50% of the time.

- 28–36: I often experience flow, certainly more times than not. My life contains many flow triggers, and I often feel my best and do my best.

- 37–45: My life is definitely organized around flow. I experience Optimal Human Performance on a daily basis, and because of this, I do my best and feel my best.

My Flow Trigger Plan

To get even more flow, I will implement the nine flow triggers into my life by taking the following clear and specific actions:

DAY 26

ASSESSMENT:
Assess Your Growth

Everyone thinks of changing the world, but no one thinks of changing himself.

—Leo Tolstoy, "Three Methods of Reform"

Congratulations, you've almost arrived at the final module. At the start of this book, I invited you to trust me—and the *Unhackable* process. I knew these thirty days would stretch you in ways you've never imagined. Day 26 is no exception. You're going to find out how much you've grown.

You'll soon share your dream with yourself and your world, in that order. For many people, this is the first time they've truly given themselves permission to dream freely without judgment or restraint.

It might feel a little odd wrapping your mind around the fact that there are no longer any borders, barriers, or boundaries. But the only limitations that exist reside within your mind and your mind alone.

In *Elixir Project*, as the main character, Aryedne, nears The Boon Ceremony, she senses a twinge of anxiety rising within her. Fear and bravery—both wrapped up in one person and fighting for dominance. It's a paradox, but sometimes the battle for the soul is won in surrender. See if you can relate:

I feel myself getting stronger. I always wanted permission to be brave. Guess I needed to be backed into a corner for it to come out.

The Boon Ceremony is just one more opportunity. If I tell the truth when the whole world's listening—who knows? That scared little girl inside may run away forever.

My hope is that this will soon be your experience too. You're about to head into the Boon Ceremony, after all—the final module. You'll have the chance to be brave and an opportunity to tell the truth. That scared little child inside of you may run away forever.

If that makes you nervous, it shouldn't.

You're ready.

You've grown these past twenty-five days.

You've felt yourself getting stronger.

You've been barreling toward your Boon and becoming Unhackable like the other brave ones who came before you. Here are a few of the messages they've sent our team. Their energy is electric:

I love this teaching. I wrote my book manuscript in 30 days by implementing these principles. I've been so much more productive in all areas of my life.

—Chris McClure

I AM FREE! Just finished going through all those Trello cards. I must have dumped 50–60 things that just keep getting shuffled around. Some have been around for several years. I no longer have so many things hanging over me.

—Laura Diehl

"Not bad" for a guy who spent the past 2 years suffering depression. My biggest takeaway: CONFIDENCE. This content has changed me. I am thankful and excited.

—Steve Baker

This past weekend, I wanted to get away to a quiet place with no Internet where I could "get into flow" and write. I did just that. I lost track of time, food, everything. I was so jazzed I could hardly sleep Saturday night. The neuro-chemicals were doing happy dances! I finished my book proposal, intro, and chapter 1!

—Terri Sullivant

Now, it's your turn.

Give yourself the gift of assessing your growth. Be pleased with how far you've come rather than focusing on how far you have left to go. Dan Sullivan advises people to measure the "gain," not the "gap." If you rush ahead thinking about the future without stopping to celebrate your present, you'll miss a major opportunity. Remember, flow is about the Deep Now. Breathe in this moment and let the gratitude follow.

CLOSE YOUR GAP DAY 26: ASSESS YOUR GROWTH

Visit UnhackableBook.com and take the Unhackability Assessment. You'll discover more about yourself and your unique personality by answering a few questions. We'll send you a *free* customized report that will provide additional clarity.

Once you get your report, you can fill in your Unhackability Score below:

Idea: _____

Focus: _____

Flow: _____

Result: _____

Some readers may want to skip this ten-minute exercise. I invite you to reconsider. Please don't proceed in the book until you've taken the Unhackability Assessment. Skipping this step only hacks you.

Once you receive your report, please compare your results with the first time you took the Assessment at the beginning of the book.

UNHACKABILITY ASSESSMENT		
CATEGORY	DAY 1	DAY 26
IDEA		
FOCUS		
FLOW		
RESULT		

Look at both sets of numbers, then answer the following questions.

1. What are your feelings about the two different assessment results?

2. Do you believe you've grown these past twenty-five days? If so, how?

3. What is your biggest takeaway from the book so far?

4. In big or small ways, how has your thinking changed?

We love to celebrate your progress. If you want our team to see your Unhackability score, please post a photo of your results from both Day 1 and Day 26 on your favorite social media channel with #UnhackableBook. Use the chart above to make it easier.

Besides cheering you on, we want to share your wins with our entire team. Each story of transformation reignites our passion for what we do—igniting souls.

And now, get ready for your Boon Ceremony.

PART 5

DAY 27

CLARIFY:
Clarify Your Boon

Knowledge will not attract money, unless it is organized, and intelligently directed, through the practical plans of action, to the definite end of accumulation of money.

—Napoleon Hill, *Think and Grow Rich*

Welcome to the first day of the fifth and final module—the Boon Ceremony. Although you can see the *finish line*, your world needs you to *finish strong*. This could be your most difficult day. It's going to require you to be mentally tough and to show up filled up.

I'll share from experience—after training thousands of people with this content, I know it's easy to let off the gas on the last lap. But doing so will only get you hacked. Be aware:

These final days are where Boons are won and lost.

One common way people let off the gas is by assuming that because they've *heard* something they've also *mastered* something. This is especially true for those with a Western mindset. It's tempting to get suckered into this, especially when it comes to speed. We want the newest and the freshest, and because we pride ourselves on going wider rather than deeper, we miss the true treasure right below the surface.

Here's an illustration. Read the following statement: "I already *know* that."

Notice the difference of perspective with the word *know*:

Ancient Greek perspective of *know* = I *heard* that
Ancient Hebrew perspective of *know* = I *live* that

Until we've mastered Unhackability, evidenced by the way we conduct our lives, we still have more learning to do.

It's a paradox. In one sense, you've received a graduate-level education in idea achievement. But in another sense, you're only at the beginning. You're now aware of a brand new world called Flawless Idea Anatomy, Deliberate Magnetic Focus, and Optimal Human Performance.

TIME TO GO EVEN DEEPER

Today—Day 27—I'm inviting you to clarify your Boon. To make this easier, we'll review and reflect upon some of your previous daily missions. This will take a little effort, but your Boon is worth it.

It's difficult for achievers to pause and reflect, but please trust me and trust the process. Days 28–30 will be much easier if you do a little digging and organize the learning you've experienced thus far. You might be thinking, *Why organize?* Here's why:

No Organization = No Boon

Don't take my word for it. Take Napoleon Hill's. Read this excerpt from his legendary book *Think and Grow Rich* several times and mine the gold. There's a payoff coming.

THERE are two kinds of knowledge. One is general, the other is specialized. General knowledge, no matter how great in quantity or variety it may be, is of but little use in the accumulation of money. The faculties of the great universities possess, in the aggregate, practically every form of general knowledge known to civilization.

Most of the professors have but little or no money. They specialize on teaching knowledge, but they do not specialize on the organization, or the use of knowledge. KNOWLEDGE will not attract money, unless it is organized, and intelligently directed, through practical PLANS OF ACTION, to the DEFINITE END of accumulation of money.

Lack of understanding of this fact has been the source of confusion to millions of people who falsely believe that "knowledge is power." It is nothing of the sort! Knowledge is only potential power. It becomes power only when, and if, it is organized into definite plans of action, and directed to a definite end.

This "missing link" in all systems of education known to civilization today, may be found in the failure of educational institutions to teach their students HOW TO ORGANIZE AND USE KNOWLEDGE AFTER THEY ACQUIRE IT.

Many people make the mistake of assuming that, because Henry Ford had but little "schooling," he is not a man of "education." Those who make this mistake do not know Henry Ford, nor do they understand the real meaning of the word "educate." That word is derived from the Latin word "educo," meaning to educe, to draw out, to DEVELOP FROM WITHIN. An educated man is not, necessarily, one who has an abundance of general or specialized knowledge.

An educated man is one who has so developed the faculties of his mind that he may acquire anything he wants, or its equivalent, without violating the rights of others.

Don't hack yourself. As I've warned, if you skip this step or this process, you'll miss out on your Boon. You're so close. Commit to maintaining your focus. Keep going, and I'll tell you where to find the information for each day. Let's do this together.

BOON RECAP

On Day 2, you picked your Boon. I said, "Nobody sees his or her Boon perfectly in the beginning. ... Clarity comes as you take action. Picking your Boon is like emerging out of a fog. Embrace the paradox: the clouds lift when you move toward your desire."

Rewrite the Boon you wrote that day:

On Day 5, you counted your cost. I said, "Be honest. What fears do you have about truly committing to your Boon?"

Rewrite the fears you had on that day:

Do those fears still scare you today? Why or why not? Write your feelings below.

On Day 6, you claimed your promise. I said, "If you want to claim a big *win*, you need to clarify a big *why*. You'll probably give up along the way if the idea is only yours. But if you understand that your idea was given *through* you and not *to* you, then you understand it's on God to open up the heavens and pour down the promises. Your job is to believe in yourself."

Rewrite the *why* you wrote that day:

On Day 10, you created your idea. I said, "The right step is always the one that requires action. Most people don't like that answer. They want clarity *before* they take action. But clarity only comes *because* we take action. The way forward is never smooth, clear, or obvious in the beginning."

You did your best to create your Boon Sheet. Rewrite it again.

On Day 11, you wrote your Boon check. I said, "Matter can exist in two places at once. ... and ideas can exist in two places at once. An idea manifests in the mind of the person imagining the thought. ... That same idea exists somewhere else in the universe simultaneously."

You wrote your Boon Check. Endorse your check one more time.

On Day 13, you established your deadline. I said, "Picking a deadline is important. It's similar to picking a destination for a road trip—without one, you're going in circles, but a deadline isn't enough. Just because you have a *destination* doesn't mean you also have a *motivation.* What gets you moving in full force is urgency. Paying a penalty for missing your deadline injects a serious dose of motivation."

You wrote your Boon Contract. Rewrite it again.

On Day 21, you silenced your critics. I said, if you're like most people, you've let one or more of these statements hack you:

I often get in my own way.
I'm my own worst enemy.
I'm self-critical.
I struggle with self-limiting beliefs.

I doubt my own abilities.
I don't see my own greatness.
I know all my weaknesses.
It's tough for me to identify my strengths.
I never finish anything.
I don't want to put something out unless it's perfect.

You discovered it was time to get out of your own way and get into flow. You wrote your Boon Poem. Rewrite it again.

CLOSE YOUR GAP DAY 27: CLARIFY YOUR BOON

Based on your Boon recap, look how far you've come. You know much more today than when you first started. Because you took action, you now have even more clarity.

Keep in mind, clarity is a tricky thing. Most people naïvely say they want it without understanding that clarity comes with a cost:

That's the danger in clarity. Once you know what you want, you're dissatisfied with anything less.

This is the point of no return. The growing clarity you've been experiencing will lead you through a series of other steps I explain in my book *The Deeper Path*. We call the process below The Deeper Path Payoff. Notice that you begin with clarity and conclude with income. That income may be measured in terms of monetary wealth or relational, spiritual, physical, or emotional wealth.

The Deeper Path Payoff

clarity   competence confidence   influence   impact   income

○ ➡ ○ ➡ ○ ➡ ○ ➡ ○ ➡ ○

Are you ready for more?

I thought so. Having completed your Boon recap, it's now time to clarify your boon. Don't aim for perfection, and remember what Steve Jobs said: "You can only connect [the dots] looking backward."

I encourage you to get in a quiet place. Create a space conducive to deep thinking. Play some Boon-clarifying music if it helps. I'll include my song of choice for this exercise. Go to YouTube and look for "As My Heart Sings" by Simon Reece.[108]

Listen to that music for at least one minute with your eyes closed before writing.

Now (as best you know how at this moment), what new insights and awareness do you have about your Boon? Please write them below.

Clarify My Boon

DAY 28

CRAFT:
Craft Your Boon

Being a comfortable public speaker, which involves easily being able to go off-script, strongly signals competence.

—Amy Cuddy

irth is messy. It has to be. No one hand delivers you a script for your dream or idea. The creative process is raw and unrefined. But this is the beauty and mystery all wrapped into one.

In *Elixir Project*, at the Boon Ceremony, Aryedne Lewis is standing before a global livestream audience, ready to address the world with her Boon Speech. She has successfully completed all three Verdicts: Flawless Idea Anatomy, Deliberate Magnetic Focus, and Optimal Human Performance. In the process, she's become a stronger version of herself, more aware of her own Unhackability. Although she's a little anxious about giving her Boon Speech, she knows the world needs to hear the truth she needs to tell.

Your Boon Speech is coming, and the world needs to hear your truth too. Remember Day 21—Self: Silence Your Critic?

Referencing Walt Whitman's poem, Mr. Keating invited Todd
Anderson to the front of the class to perform a barbaric yawp.
Read this excerpt from Whitman's poem:

"Song of Myself" from *Leaves of Grass*

I loafe and invite my soul,
I lean and loafe at my ease observing a spear of summer grass.

...

The past and present wilt—I have fill'd them, emptied them,
And proceed to fill my next fold of the future.

...

The spotted hawk swoops by and accuses me, he com-
plains of my gab and my loitering.

I too am not a bit tamed—I too am untranslatable;
I sound my barbaric yawp over the roofs of the world.

The last scud of day holds back for me,
It flings my likeness after the rest and true as any on the
shadow'd wilds,
It coaxes me to the vapor and the dusk.

I depart as air, I shake my white locks at the runaway sun,
I effuse my flesh in eddies, and drift it in lacy jags.

I bequeath myself to the dirt to grow from the grass I love,
If you want me again, look for me under your boot-soles.

Literary critics agree that "Whitman's yawp is the release of
the 'kosmos' within him."[109] In our context, this is a reference

to his Boon. Before you're dirt, while you still have air in your lungs, you have the opportunity to sound your barbaric yawp over the rooftops of the world.

In Day 29, you'll have the chance to communicate your Boon to the world. Like Todd's poem and Aryedne's speech, it may be unpolished and imperfect, but that's exactly what we're looking for. As George Patton said, "A good plan violently executed now is better than a perfect plan next week."

The key is to take imperfect action, and this might even mean *going off script*.

There are times to stick to the script. This is not one of them. Your Boon is intended to disrupt—all flawless ideas do.

FOLLOW YOUR OWN SCRIPT

In the movie *Walk the Line*, Johnny Cash stuck to the script—at least in the beginning.[110] Although his passion was music, he settled for going door-to-door trying to sell products he didn't believe in. Despite exerting effort, he was miserable and failing miserably—not a good combo.

Finally, he met a man named Sam Phillips who gave him a chance to audition. This was his big moment. But rather than singing his own song, he stuck to the script and sang somebody else's. Thankfully, Sam interrupted him.

Unpacking a few lines of dialogue will help you as you prepare to craft your Boon.

Sam: I don't record material that doesn't sell, Mr. Cash ... and gospel like that doesn't sell.

People crave authenticity. Now, more than ever, we can tell the difference. We can spot imposters—those going through the motions—from a mile away.

Johnny: Was it the gospel or the way I sing it?

I believe Johnny's question was sincere. We can get to a point where we're so used to suppressing, performing, and posturing that we forget our own voice.

Sam: Both.

Johnny's audio and video didn't match. This is true for many people today. Their words don't match their actions. Part of Johnny's problem was his song, and part of his problem was his singing. Both were forgettable, and neither evoked emotion.

Johnny: Well, what's wrong with the way I sing it?

Johnny asked clarifying questions. He was hungry for change. However, transformation requires action, too, not only instruction.

Sam: I don't believe you.

As if a bullet had ripped through his facade, Johnny had nowhere to hide. He was exposed for the imposter he was.

Johnny: You saying I don't believe in God?

When we're called out, we often try a diversion to elude the truth. We can change the subject or attack the source. But this tactic never leads to life change.

Band Member: J.R., come on, let's go.

Johnny: No. I want to understand. I mean, we come down here, we play for a minute ... and he tells me I don't believe in God.

Johnny was tired of pretending. Besides, he didn't have any other truth-tellers in his life. He pushed back to see how far Sam would go.

Sam: You know exactly what I'm telling you. We've already heard that song a hundred times ... just like that, just like how you sang it.

Sam didn't back down. The line had been drawn—now the question was, would Johnny walk it?

Johnny: Well, you didn't let us bring it home.

The victim took one final stand. Blame. Excuses. Denial. Johnny had made his BED, and he wasn't about to get out of it.

Sam: Bring ... bring it home? All right, let's bring it home. If you was hit by a truck and you were lying out in that gutter dying, and you had time to sing one song—huh— one song people would remember before you're dirt, one song that would let God know what you felt about your time here on earth, one song that would sum you up—you tellin' me that's the song you'd sing? That same Jimmie Davis tune we hear on the radio all day? About your peace within and how it's real and how you're gonna shout it?

Or would you sing something different? Something real, something you felt? Because I'm telling you right now, that's the kind of song people want to hear. That's the kind of song that truly saves people.

It ain't got nothing to do with believing in God, Mr. Cash. It has to do with believing in yourself.

Sam yanked the script right out of Johnny's head. The only option was for Johnny to sing one from his heart.

Johnny: Well, I've got a couple songs I wrote in the Air Force. You got anything against the Air Force?

Sam: No.

Johnny: I do.

Johnny was holding back all this time. He had his own script tucked away deep inside. Although he'd written it years ago, he'd never had the courage to go off script—until now.

Band Member: J.R., whatever you're about to play, we ain't never heard it.

Sam didn't know what was coming, and neither did the band. Still, the result was magic. Johnny's band caught on to the melody, and they joined in singing his song too. By going off script, he scored a record deal and achieved his Boon.

GOING OFF SCRIPT

In my mind, the script is

- a metaphor for blind conformity
- a mold the world tries to squeeze each one of us into
- a prison of the mind whose bars are defined by a Boonless existence

Like Johnny, I've had my moments of truth. At different times in my life, I've had to decide: would I stick to the script or go off script?

- I was told to stick to the script and serve in a foreign country as a missionary. I never returned to Papua New Guinea after my two-month term because I didn't feel like it was my calling.

- Nobody in my family ever went to graduate school. I went off script and earned a master's degree.

- I was told that writing a book was selfish. I went off script and wrote seven books and counting.

- The church I served didn't value advanced degrees. I went off script and earned my doctorate.

- Close friends and family members warned me not to leave my comfortable day job because I had a wife and three small kids. I went off script, followed my passion, and started my dream job.

- I'm the son of two parents who made their careers in the nonprofit world. I went off script, left the pastorate, and entered the business world.

- I was told there are only two publishing models: selfpublishing and traditional publishing. I went off script and started my own global publishing company built around a third publishing model: Author Academy Elite (AuthorAcademyElite.com). We've disrupted the industry.

- Colleagues advised me to stick to the script and continue writing nonfiction books. I wrote a young adult nearfuture thriller.

- Naysayers told me I could never turn a fiction book into a conference. I went off script and created a soldout Igniting Souls Conference centered on becoming Unhackable.

- Doubters told me building a course around a fiction book was impossible. We created ElixirProjectExperience.com, and it's changed the lives of thousands of people.

I've never regretted going off script. To me, it's the natural path of becoming Unhackable and achieving your Boon. This doesn't mean it's not scary. Of course it is. But it's always worth it.

CLOSE YOUR GAP DAY 28: CRAFT YOUR BOON

This daily mission is your moment of truth.

You'll always have naysayers and doubters trying to make you stick to the script. Sometimes your strongest resistance comes from the lips of loved ones. They mean well and don't want to see you get hurt. Their desire is for you to be safe and do the right thing. But sometimes, the right thing is to go off script.

It's your choice, and it's your life. Today, as you craft your Boon, you'll have to decide which script to write—the one they *want* you to write or the one you know you *need* to write.

Please craft your Boon below. Think of it as a Boon Speech you'll share with the world. The truth is you may share it sooner than you think. (Keep it to five minutes or less.)

I'll paraphrase Sam Phillip's exhortation to get you started:

If you was hit by a truck and you were lying out in that gutter dying, and you had time to give one Boon Speech—huh—one speech people would remember before you're dirt, one speech that would let God know what you felt about your time here on earth, one speech that would sum you up, would you say something different? Something real, something you felt? Because I'm telling you right now, that's the kind of Boon Speech people want to hear.

My Boon Speech

DAY 29

COMMUNICATE:
Communicate Your Boon

*Live every day as if it were your last because someday
you're going to be right.*

—Muhammad Ali

What I'm about to say won't shock you. Still, it's a truth most people don't want to hear. In fact, it's a truth many people spend their whole life running from.

Ready for it? Drum roll please ...

You're going to die.

Ouch! The Hallmark channel wouldn't approve of starting off a chapter this way. However, you and I have been brutally honest throughout this book. We began our conversation about Unhackability this way, and it's essential we maintain our candor as we near the end of this book.

The reality is, none of us is going to make it out of here alive. We hear this theme from modern-day musicians like Eminem (in "Lose Yourself"):

If you had one shot to seize everything you ever wanted
… Would you capture it or just let it slip?

And we read it in the Roman poet Horace's *Odes* in 23 BC
when he first used the phrase *carpe diem*, translated

Seize the day.

Look anywhere, and you'll see it in lyrics, literature, sermons, and films. We're all going to die. You've known it your entire life, and so have I. The more relevant question is, *How does this reality shape us while we're still alive?*

This book is not morbid. Quite the opposite, actually. It's a celebration of life—therefore, it recognizes the relationship between life and death.

If you want your time to count, you must count your time. Urgency!

There it is again. You don't have forever on this planet, and neither do I. This was Sam Phillips' challenge to Johnny Cash—you have one song to sing before you're dirt.

It doesn't matter if you're nine years old or ninety-nine. If you're breathing, your Boon is still possible. Look at Diana Nyad if you think you're too old. Look at Kyle Maynard if you think you're too unqualified. Now is the time to focus on action, not excuses. Now is the time for you to communicate your Boon.

TELL US WHAT YOU KNOW

In *Elixir Project*, at Aryedne's Boon Ceremony, the stakes for telling the truth were extremely high. She knew her life was on the line, but it didn't hold her back:

> *"Senior Board of Clerics, proxies, and global citizens, it's my honor to address you tonight," I say with as much poise as*

I can muster. "When I began the Project, I had my doubts about myself, my fellow clerics, and even ELIXIR. But throughout the Verdicts, over these past three days, I discovered the truth."

"Regarding myself, I discovered that fear is a necessary part of life, and that when it counts most, I need to trust my gut— and listen to my heart."

"Regarding my fellow clerics, I discovered we're flawed, each of us. And that being honest bonds us together, when we don't know the right answers—or even the correct questions."

"And finally I discovered the truth about ELIXIR."

"My uncle Cai said it best. Recently, he warned me."

"He said, 'They're watching us.' I wondered, Who's watching?"

"He said, 'Things aren't always what they seem.' I wondered, What things?"

"And finally he said, 'Don't believe what you think; believe what you know.'"

"So here I am—invited to tell you what I know."

What happens next is her moment of truth. Aryedne communicates her Boon. Your stakes—though different—are just as high. Although your life might not be on the line, your legacy is. And what you do next—to quote Marcus Aurelius—"echoes in eternity."

CLOSE YOUR GAP DAY 29: COMMUNICATE YOUR BOON

It's time to communicate your Boon. Just like Todd's poem and Aryedne's speech, it may be unpolished and imperfect, but that's exactly what we're looking for. The key is to take imperfect action.

This day is intentionally shorter than some of the others because you and your Boon are the focus. I'm giving you plenty of time to communicate your Boon.

I invite you to record yourself giving your Boon Speech. You can do this easily on your phone. After recording, post it on social media with #UnhackableBoonSpeech

You're not alone. We're ready to celebrate your newfound clarity and bravery. Ready or not, this your moment of truth.

UNHACKABLE BOON SPEECH PROCESS

1. Record your speech.

2. Post your speech online.

Don't believe what you think.
Believe what you know.
#UnhackableBoonSpeech

DAY 30

CREATION:
Create Your Boon

*Every dream is created twice. The first creation is mental.
Every invention, every business, every building, every painting
is conceived in the right-brain imagination first. ...
The second creation is physical.*

—Mark Batterson

Welcome to Day 30—Creation—your *final* day. Ironically, it's also your *first* day. We've come full circle. If you recall, Day 10 was also titled "Creation." This is intentional.

All ideas are created twice, mentally and physically—first creation and second creation. Both exist simultaneously, and when you're Unhackable, the time and space it takes to manifest your idea are irrelevant.

Remember where we started—by defining *abracadabra*. There's no gap between ideation and implementation. Rather, abracadabra literally means:

It came to pass as it was spoken.
I create as I speak.

This is the power of Unhackability. As you master these thirty missions, you'll rinse and repeat this process again and again. You'll imagine your Boon and then implement your Boon. And it won't stop there. You'll be entrusted with a new Boon and then engage in Flawless Idea Anatomy, Deliberate Magnetic Focus, and Optimal Human Performance all over again.

Never forget your divine birthright. You've been created to create, and when you do, you're literally fulfilling your God-given calling. But the opposite is true as well. When you get hacked, you choose your humanity over divinity.

It's easy to tell the difference. Look no further than your level of enthusiasm for your work and life. If you lack true enthusiasm, you're being fueled by a source other than the divine. Duty? Guilt? Shame? Revenge? Spite? Or something else? That's for you to determine, not me.

But when you're fueled by enthusiasm—literally meaning "possessed by God"—then you're Unhackable. *Nothing* can stop you, and *no one* can stand against you.

THE RISK IS WORTH IT

Many times, we stress over what everyone else will think of us if we pursue our Boon. The truth is no one is thinking of us when it comes to our Boon. They're all too focused on themselves. True thinkers, poets, scientists, artists, and filmmakers understand this better than most.

One of my favorite films released in 2011. *The Tree of Life* was categorized as an experimental film. This American epic drama written and directed by Terrence Malick "chronicles the origins and meaning of life by way of a middle-aged man's childhood memories of his family living in 1950s Texas, interspersed with imagery of the origins of the known universe and the inception of life on Earth."[111]

In January 2012, it was nominated for three Academy Awards—Best Picture, Best Director, and Best Cinematography. Although many critics loved it, others absolutely hated it.

> *The New Yorker* said a "seraphic strain" in Malick's work "hits a solipsistic high" in *The Tree of Life.* "While the result will sound to some like a prayer, others may find it increasingly lonely and locked, and may themselves pray for Ben Hecht or Billy Wilder to rise from the dead and attack Malick's script with a quiver of poisonous wisecracks."[112]

> Sukhdev Sandhu, chief film critic of *The Daily Telegraph*, describes the movie as "self-absorbed" and "achingly slow, almost buckling under the weight of its swoony poetry."[113]

> Lee Marshall's review for *Screen Daily* followed a similar line, seeing the film as "a cinematic credo about spiritual transcendence which, while often shot through with poetic yearning, preaches too directly to its audience."[114] Stephanie Zacharek of *Movieline* praised the technical aspects of the film, such as the "gorgeous photography," however, she states that nonetheless, it is "a gargantuan work of pretension and cleverly concealed self-absorption."[115]

> Filmmaker David Lynch said that, while he liked Malick's previous works, *The Tree of Life* "wasn't my cup of tea."[116]

These responses are familiar to all people who pursue their Boons. Creating your Boon will involve risks. It will also evoke mixed reviews.

- Some will ignore you.

- Some will critique you.

- Some will applaud you.

Regardless of the responses, creating your Boon is essential. It's a gift from heaven above that reflects your time on earth below. Your path will include twists and turns, and you'll face resistance. But in the end, it will be worth it.

Don't get caught up on *time* or *timing*. By now, you know time is simply a temporary measurement chockfull of limitations. Don't wait for the perfect connections or the perfect resources to take action and start creating your Boon. The Law of Diminishing Intent coined by Jim Rohn is real: "The longer you wait to take action, the less likely you are to take action."

CREATE THE SPECTACLE

We'll end our conversation by examining a work of art. The creator is Sue Austin. You can read my short description of her Boon, or you can watch it for yourself. I'll warn you ahead of time: My words do her dream an injustice. How can you describe a woman in a wheelchair scuba diving?

I encourage you to visit her Boon on YouTube. Search for "Creating the Spectacle! Online - Part 1 - Finding Freedom."[117]

The first time I watched it, I couldn't take my eyes off the screen. The otherworldly music combined with an unimaginable scene mesmerized me. In that moment, I realized my only Boon limitations are the ones that exist inside my mind.

Think about all the obstacles Sue Austin faced when trying to implement her idea. I'm sure, at times, contemplating her Boon felt overwhelming. She needed

- scuba training

- a modified wheelchair

- a film crew

- funding

- publicity

And this is only the beginning. Her list went on and on. She could have easily been hacked and given up.

The truth is, you and I can relate. Whenever we seriously consider our Boons, all we see are the obstacles in front of us.

This used to *frustrate* me. Today, it *fuels* me. Observing all these obstacles is a good thing and a necessary step in Boon achievement. Dan Sullivan tells us why: "All those things that seem to oppose our goals are actually the raw material for achieving them."[118]

BOON OBSTACLES = BOON OPPORTUNITIES

Obstacles are important because they serve as clues for achieving your Boon. By changing your perspective, they shift from obstacles to opportunities.

With this new perspective, review Sue's list and notice the action steps that emerge:

- *Scuba training* = Get certified.

- *A modified wheelchair* = Contact wheelchair makers with a proposal for sponsorship.

- *A film crew* = Reach out to the film crew that did an artistic film to raise awareness for other charities.

- *Funding* = Write a grant. Pursue wealthy donors impacted by a loved one in a wheelchair.

- *Publicity* = Write a press release and invite reporters to the filming.

I'm not sure that these are the exact actions Sue took, but I know without a doubt she overcame her obstacles.

I've used this strategy for every Boon I've achieved. First, I make a long list of every obstacle standing in my way. Then, I write down the opportunity on the other side of each obstacle. One at a time, I overcome these obstacles and move closer to my Boon.

This isn't a trendy tactic, but a battle-tested mantra birthed out of ancient stoicism as summed up in this quotation from Marcus Aurelius: "The impediment to action advances action. What stands in the way becomes the way."

Today, truth seekers are revisiting this sage advice updated for a new generation by popular writer Ryan Holiday. He condensed it down to "the obstacle is the way," also the title of his bestselling book.

On that note, it's time to identify the obstacles that will become *the way* and the path to achieving your Boon.

CLOSE YOUR GAP DAY 30: CREATE YOUR BOON

Do some deep reflection in a quiet space. Don't judge or edit. Taking notes on a physical piece of paper is ideal. If you use your phone or tablet to capture your thoughts, don't get hacked by notifications, texts, or calls. Just enable airplane mode and list of all the obstacles that stand in your way.

Boon Obstacles

Now, turn each obstacle into an opportunity. List a clear, productive action you need to take.

Boon Opportunities

Your Next Best Step

This list of obstacles—now turned into opportunities—is your next best step. If you need help along the way, we're here for you. Our team and community exist to support you and ignite your soul. Since many people inquire, I'll include a few of the most common ways we help others in their journey in the following pages. Bottom line, please reach out. We'd love to come alongside you as you create your Boon.

One Simple Request

Now that you've discovered Unhackability, I leave you with one simple request. It's obvious this message isn't mine. This idea came *through* me, not *to* me. As a result, I ask you to do something required for any idea to expand:

Spread it.
Share the message of Unhackability with others.
Your world needs you and your Boon implemented.

It's time to close the gap between dreaming and doing. It's time for you to become ...

UNHACKABLE.

If I win my Boon, my life might be abnormal forever and in the best way possible.
—Aryedne Lewis, *Elixir Project*

APPENDICES

NOTES

1 Whitman, Walt. "Song of Myself." *Leaves of Grass.*
   Self-published, 1855.

2 Winnick, Michael. "Putting a Finger on Our Phone Obsession."
   dscout. Accessed April 8, 2020. https://blog.dscout.com/
   mobile-touches.

3 Loder, Vanessa. "Why Multi-Tasking Is Worse Than Marijuana
   for Your IQ." Forbes. *Forbes Magazine,* July 16, 2014.
   https://www.forbes.com/sites/vanessaloder/2014/06/11/
   why-multi-tasking-is-worse-than-marijuana-for-your-iq/#261a6
   36c7c11.

4 Jag. "How To Watch Netflix On TV," March 29, 2020. https://
   www.reelnreel.com/watch-netflix-on-tv/.

5 Story, Louise. "Anywhere the Eye Can See, It's Likely to See
   an Ad." The New York Times. *The New York Times,* January
   15, 2007. https://www.nytimes.com/2007/01/15/business/
   media/15everywhere.html.

6 Lang, Susan S. "'Mindless Autopilot' Drives People to
   Dramatically Underestimate How Many Daily Food Decisions
   They Make, Cornell Study Finds." *Cornell Chronicle,*
   December 22, 2006. https://news.cornell.edu/stories/2006/12/
   mindless-autopilot-drives-people-underestimate-food-decisions.

7 "What Is the Name of *Star Wars* Fans?" Jedi Council Forums.
   Accessed April 9, 2020. https://boards.theforce.net/threads/
   what-is-the-name-of-star-wars-fans.27237486/.

8   Lewis, Sophie. "Lightsaber Dueling Has Become an
     Official Sport in France." CBS News. CBS Interactive,
     February 19, 2019. https://www.cbsnews.com/news/
     lightsaber-dueling-now-official-sport-france/.

9   *Star Wars* Origins—Joseph Campbell and the Hero's Journey.
     Accessed April 9, 2020. http://www.moongadget.com/origins/
     myth.html.

10   "Culprit." Accessed May 8, 2020. https://www.
     merriam-webster.com/dictionary/culprit.

11   Leroy, Sophie. "Why Is It So Hard to Do My Work? The
     Challenge of Attention Residue When Switching between
     Work Tasks." Organizational Behavior and Human Decision
     Processes. Academic Press, May 23, 2009. https://www.
     sciencedirect.com/science/article/abs/pii/S0749597809000399.

12   Nin, Anaïs and Anita Jarczok. *Seduction of the Minotaur.*
     Athens, OH: Swallow Press/Ohio University Press, 2014.

13   Hyman, Ira E. "Remembering the Future." Psychology
     Today. Sussex Publishers, June 17, 2013. https://www.
     psychologytoday.com/us/blog/mental-mishaps/201306/
     remembering-the-future.

14   M, Mateusz. "Resiliency—Motivational Video." YouTube
     Video, 2:09, July 15, 2015. https://www.youtube.com/
     watch?v=UNQhuFL6CWg.

15   Lukas Kaeonin. "Lindsey Stirling America's Got Talent."
     April 27, 2012. Video, 7:29. https://www.youtube.com/
     watch?v=M2xL7D5lPAk.

16   Moraski, Lauren. "'America's Got Talent' Asked Lindsey
     Stirling to Compete Again. Here's What She Said." HuffPost.
     HuffPost. December 20, 2018. https://www.huffpost.com/entry/
     lindsey-stirling-americas-got-talent_n_5c1941ffe4b0432554c4fe6e.

17   Fueled By Ramen. "twenty one pilots: Ode to Sleep [OFFICIAL
     VIDEO]." YouTube Video, 6:25, December 31, 2014. https://
     www.youtube.com/watch?v=2OnO3UXFZdE.

18   Hutchison, Courtney. "Armless, Legless Man to
     Climb Mount Kilimanjaro." *ABC News.* October 13,

2011. https://abcnews.go.com/Health/WellnessNews/
armless-legless-man-climb-mount-kilimanjaro-prosthetic-limbs/
story?id=14731056.

19 Estep, Kyle. "Kyle Maynard's Next Adventure:
Kilimanjaro." Gwinnett Daily Post. *Gwinnett Daily Post.*
November 11, 2011. https://www.gwinnettdailypost.
com/archive/kyle-maynard-s-next-adventure-kilimanjaro/
article_007d2e03-94c6-5e00-a045-46f36ab1b5c7.html.

20 Dorong, Desiree. "Man Born Without Hands and
Feet Climbed Two of the Highest Peaks in the World!"
Crossmap Story. Accessed July 6, 2020. https://story.
crossmap.com/man-born-without-hands-and-fee
t-climbed-two-of-the-highest-peaks-in-the-world-definitely-t
here-is-no-excuses-in-dreaming-high/.

21 Azuz, Carl. "Record-Breaking Cold Hits America; Near
Record Floods Swamp Venice; Athlete Embodies 'No
Excuses'; Objective Look at the U.S. Political Divide."
CNN. November 14, 2019. http://transcripts.cnn.com/
TRANSCRIPTS/1911/14/sn.01.html.

22 Merali, Zeeya. "Quantum 'Spookiness' Passes Toughest
Test Yet." Nature. *Nature, International Weekly Journal of
Science.* August 27, 2015. https://www.nature.com/news/
quantum-spookiness-passes-toughest-test-yet-1.18255.

23 MuonRay. "Overview of Quantum Entanglement—Einstein
Versus Bohr." MuonRay. *Science, Technology, Investigation,
Experimentation and Visualization: Irradiate Yourself with
MuonRay.* September, 8, 2014. http://muonray.blogspot.
com/2014/09/overview-of-quantum-entanglement.html

24 "Write Yourself a Check." CBN. *CBN.* Accessed May 17, 2020.
https://www1.cbn.com/700club/write-yourself-check.

25 Vance, Mike and Diane Deacon. *Think Out of the Box.* Career
Pr Inc, 1997.

26 Luke 22:44

27 John 17:24

28 Jobs, Steve. "'You've Got to Find What You Love,' Jobs Says." Stanford. *Stanford News.* June 12, 2005. https://news.stanford. edu/2005/06/14/jobs-061505/.

29 Khanna, Parag and Karan Khemka. "The coronavirus butterfly effect: Six predictions for a new world order." Fast Company. April 14, 2020. https://www.fastcompany. com/90488665/the-coronavirus-butterfly-effect-six-prediction s-for-a-new-world-order.

30 Russel Schilling, David. "Knowledge Doubling Every 12 Months, Soon to be Every 12 Hours." *Industry Tap.* April 19, 2013. https://www.industrytap. com/knowledge-doubling-every-12-months-soo n-to-be-every-12-hours/3950.

31 Lodestar Solutions. "How Fast Is Knowledge Doubling?" Accessed July 6, 2020. https://lodestarsolutions.com/ keeping-up-with-the-surge-of-information-and-human-kno wledge/.

32 Siegler, MG. "Eric Schmidt: Every 2 Days We Create As Much Information As We Did Up to 2003." TechCrunch. August 4, 2010. https://techcrunch.com/2010/08/04/schmidt-data/.

33 Russel Schilling, David. "Knowledge Doubling Every 12 Months, Soon to be Every 12 Hours."

34 Weinschenk, Ph.D., Susan. "Why We're All Addicted to Texts, Twitter and Google." *Psychology Today.* September 11, 2012. https://www.psychologytoday.com/us/blog/brain-wise/201209/ why-were-all-addicted-texts-twitter-and-google.

35 "25 Surprising Facts About Phone Addiction." Addiction Tips. February 22, 2015. https://www.addictiontips.net/ phone-addiction/phone-addiction-facts/

36 "'Phantom vibration syndrome' common in cellphone users." *CBS News.* January 12, 2016. https://www.cbsnews.com/news/ phantom-vibration-syndrome-common-in-cellphone-users/.

37 Van Camp, Jeffrey. "New study: Average teen sends 3,339 texts every month." Digital Trends. October 15, 2010. https://www. digitaltrends.com/mobile/new-study-average-teen-sends-333 9-texts-every-month/.

[38] Keating, Lauren. "Survey Finds Most People Check Their Smartphones Before Getting Out Of Bed In The Morning." *Tech Times.* March 2, 2017. https://www.techtimes.com/articles/199967/20170302/survey-finds-people-check-smartphones-before-getting-out-of-bed.htm.

[39] Keating, Lauren. "Survey Finds Most People Check Their Smartphones Before Getting Out Of Bed In The Morning."

[40] Price, Rob. "1 in 3 people check their smartphones in the middle of the night." *Insider.* September 26, 2016. https://amp.insider.com/1-in-3-people-check-smartphones-night-deloitte-study-2016-9.

[41] Manglik, Rohit. *IGNOU OPENMAT Entrance Exam 2020.* Lucknow, India: EduGorilla, 2020.

[42] Archer, M.D., Dale. "Smartphone Addiction." *Psychology Today.* July 25, 2013. https://www.psychologytoday.com/us/blog/reading-between-the-headlines/201307/smartphone-addiction.

[43] Elmore, Tim. "Nomophobia: A Rising Trend in Students." *Psychology Today.* September 18, 2014. https://www.psychologytoday.com/us/blog/artificial-maturity/201409/nomophobia-rising-trend-in-students.

[44] Grothaus, Michael. "What Happened When I Gave Up My Smartphone For A Week." Fast Company. July 21, 2016. https://www.fastcompany.com/3061913/what-happened-when-i-gave-up-my-smartphone-for-a-week.

[45] McClear, Sheila. "This exact percentage of people regularly bring their phones into the bathroom." Ladders: Fast on Your Feet. November 21, 2019. https://www.theladders.com/career-advice/this-exact-percentage-of-people-regularly-bring-their-phones-into-the-bathroom.

[46] Murphy, Samantha. "1 in 10 Americans Use Smartphones During Sex." Mashable. July 11, 2013. https://mashable.com/2013/07/11/smartphones-during-sex/.

[47] Rodriguez, Salvador. "Most adults always have smartphone nearby, 1 in 10 use it during sex." *Los Angeles Times.* July 11, 2013. https://www.latimes.com/business/technology/

la-fi-tn-smartphone-nearby-1-in-10-use-during-sex-20130711-story.html

48 Howard, Laken. "How Many Americans Choose Their Phone Over Sex." Bustle. July 20, 2016. https://www.bustle.com/art icles/173347-nearly-one-in-three-americans-wo uld-rathergive-up-sex-than-their-smartphone.

49 Rodriguez, Salvador. "Most adults always have smartphone nearby, 1 in 10 use it during sex."

50 Ibid.

51 Penn State University. "Cell Phones Are Controlling Our Lives." January 28, 2016. https://sites.psu.edu/taylorariety/2016/01/28/cell-phones-are-controlling-our-lives/.

52 NPR Staff. "In A World That's Always On, We Are Trapped In The 'Present.'" NPR. March 25, 2013. https://www.npr.org/2013/03/25/175056313/in-a-world-thats-always-o n-we-are-trapped-in-the-present.

53 FireMetalMan. "Digiphrenia." Urban Dictionary. March 12, 2017. https://www.urbandictionary.com/define.php?term=digiphrenia.

54 Fisher, MD, Robert E. "'Digiphrenia'—Coping with Digital Information Overload." ASCO Connection. September 25, 2013. https://connection.asco.org/blogs/%E2%80%9Cdigiphr enia%E2%80%9D%E2%80%94coping-digital-information-o verload.

55 Ducharme, Jamie. "'Phubbing' Is Hurting Your Relationships. Here's What It Is." Time. March 29, 2018. https://time.com/5216853/what-is-phubbing/

56 Wikipedia. "Phubbing." Accessed June 25, 2020. https://en.wikipedia.org/wiki/Phubbing.

57 Ducharme, Jamie. "'Phubbing' Is Hurting Your Relationships. Here's What It Is."

58 World of Buzz. "Man Who Was Staring At His Phone Died From Walking Off A Cliff." December 27, 2015. https://worldofbuzz.com/man-who-was-staring-at-hi s-phone-died-from-walking-off-a-cliff/

59   Edgar Snyder & Associates. "Texting and Driving Accident Statistics." Accessed June 25, 2020. https://www. edgarsnyder.com/car-accident/cause-of-accident/cell-phone/ cell-phone-statistics.html.

60   Stewart Law Offices. "Is Texting While Driving as Dangerous as Drunk Driving?" October 3, 2018. https://www. stewartlawoffices.net/is-texting-while-driving-as-dangerou s-as-drunk-driving/.

61   Parkinson, Cyril Northcote. "Parkinson's Law." *The Economist.* November 19, 1955. https://www.economist.com/ news/1955/11/19/parkinsons-law.

62   'Falconer, Joel. "How to Use Parkinson's Law to Your Advantage." Lifehack. Accessed June 25, 2020. https://www. lifehack.org/articles/featured/how-to-use-parkinsons-law-t o-your-advantage.html

63   Covey, Stephen. *The 7 Habits of Highly Effective People: Powerful Lessons in Personal Change.* New York, NY: Simon & Schuster, 2013.

64   Tracy, Brian. "Make Every Minute Count." Brian Tracy International. Accessed June 25, 2020. https://www.briantracy. com/blog/business-success/make-every-minute-count/.

65   *Kary Oberbrunner Podcast.* https://karyoberbrunner.com/podcast.

66   Leroy, Sophie. "Why Is It so Hard to Do My Work? The Challenge of Attention Residue When Switching between Work Tasks." *Organizational Behavior and Human Decision Processes* 109, no. 2 (2009): 168–81. https://doi.org/10.1016/j. obhdp.2009.04.002.

67   MindTools. "Cognitive Load Theory: Helping People Learn Effectively." Accessed July 6, 2020. https://www.mindtools.com/ pages/article/cognitive-load-theory.htm.

68   Krockow, Ph.D., Eva. "How Many Decisions Do We Make Each Day?" *Psychology Today.* September 27, 2018. https:// www.psychologytoday.com/us/blog/stretching-theory/201809/ how-many-decisions-do-we-make-each-day.

69 Williams, Ray. "How Neuroscience Can Help Us Make Better Decisions." Ray Williams. Accessed June 25, 2020. https://raywilliams.ca/neuroscience-can-help-us-make-better-decisions/.

70 Lewis, Michael. "Obama's Way." *Vanity Fair.* September 11, 2012. https://www.vanityfair.com/news/2012/10/michael-lewis-profile-barack-obama.

71 Oberbrunner, Kary. "OPUS." Kary Oberbrunner. Accessed June 25, 2020. https://karyoberbrunner.com/opus. OPUS was created by Chet Scott of BuiltToLead.com

72 Sullivan, Dan. "Strategic Coach Workshop." Toronto, Canada. Strategic Coach. Workshop Lecture, January 13, 2020.

73 The Oracles. "Warren Buffet Says the Secret to Success Is Saying 'No.' Do Experts Agree?" *Money.* May 8, 2019. https://money.com/warren-buffett-says-no-to-everything/.

74 Built to Lead. https://builttolead.com/.

75 Ryan, Tom. *Chosen Suffering: Becoming Elite in Life and Leadership.* Powell, OH: Author Academy Elite, 2020. This quote taken from the book and an interview with the author.

76 Wikipedia. "Sensory overload." Accessed June 25, 2020. https://en.wikipedia.org/wiki/Sensory_overload.

77 Stevens, Susan and Wayne A. Hening. *Textbook of Clinical Neurology.* Amsterdam, Netherlands: Elsevier, 2007.

78 DiSalvo, David. "Your Brain Sees Even When You Don't." *Forbes.* June 22, 2013. https://www.forbes.com/sites/daviddisalvo/2013/06/22/your-brain-sees-even-when-you-dont/#16a66a8d116a.

79 Encyclopaedia Britannica. "Physiology." Accessed June 25, 2020. https://www.britannica.com/science/information-theory/Physiology.

80 Hill, Napoleon. *Think and Grow Rich.* Shippensburg, PA: Sound Wisdom, 1937.

81 Proverbs 23:7 NASB.

82 Radparvar, Dave. "Neurons that fire together, wire together." Holstee. Accessed June 25, 2020. https://www.holstee.com/

blogs/mindful-matter/neurons-that-fire-together-wire-together#
:~:text=%E2%80%9CNeurons%20that%20fire%20together%
2C%20wire,gratitude%20can%20be%20so%20powerful.
&text=Neuropsychologist%20Donald%20Hebb%20first%20
used,formed%20and%20reinforced%20through%20repetition.

83 Orenstein, Hannah. "These Horrifyingly Messy
Desktops Will Give You So Much Anxiety." *Seventeen.*
July 26, 2017. https://www.seventeen.com/life/
a10359190/these-horrifyingly-messy-desktops-will-giv
e-you-so-much-anxiety/.

84 Stokes, Natasha. "15 Reasons Why Your Computer is Slow."
Techlicious. April 4, 2019. https://www.techlicious.com/tip/
reasons-why-your-computer-is-slow/.

85 Oberbrunner, Kary. *The Deeper Path.* Powell, OH: Author
Academy Elite, 2018.

86 Tierney, John. "The Advantages of Closing a Few Doors." *The
New York Times.* February 26, 2008. https://www.nytimes.
com/2008/02/26/science/26tier.html.

87 Nin, Anaïs. *Seduction of the Minotaur.* Chicago, IL: 1973.

88 Allen, James. *The Complete Works of James Allen.* Prague, Czech
Republic: e-artnow, 2019.

89 Hill, Napoleon. *Think and Grow Rich.* Shippensburg, PA:
Sound Wisdom, 1937.

90 Asprey, Dave. "Transcript of 'The Rise of Superman
with Steven Kotler.'" *Bulletproof: The State of High
Performance.* Podcast transcript, April 1, 2014. https://
blog.daveasprey.com/wp-content/uploads/2014/04/
Transcript-109-The-Rise-of-Superman-with-Steven-Kotler.pdf.

91 Johns Hopkins Medical Institutions. "This Is Your Brain
On Jazz: Researchers Use MRI To Study Spontaneity,
Creativity." ScienceDaily. www.sciencedaily.com/
releases/2008/02/080226213431.htm (accessed June 27, 2020).

92 Geirland, John. "Go With The Flow." *Wired.* September 1,
1996. https://www.wired.com/1996/09/czik/.

93 Couric, Katie. "Capt. Sully Worried About Airline Industry." *CBS News.* February 10, 2009. https://www.cbsnews.com/news/capt-sully-worried-about-airline-industry/.

94 Weir, Peter. *Dead Poets Society.* June 2, 1989. Burbank, CA: Touchstone Pictures.

95 Harvard Business Review, Karen Dillon, Amy Gallo. *HBR Guides to Emotional Intelligence at Work Collection.* Boston, MA: Harvard Business Review Press, 2017.

96 Hampton, Debbie. "Neuroplasticity: The 10 Fundamentals Of Rewiring Your Brain." Reset.me. October 28, 2015. https://reset.me/story/neuroplasticity-the-10-fundamentals-of-rewiring-your-brain/.

97 Cambridge University. "Brain activity in sex addiction mirrors that of drug addiction." Accessed July 2, 2020. https://www.cam.ac.uk/research/news/brain-activity-in-sex-addiction-mirrors-that-of-drug-addiction

98 Kotler, Steven. "Is The Secret To Ultimate Human Performance The F-Word?" *Forbes.* January 8, 2014. https://www.forbes.com/sites/stevenkotler/2014/01/08/the-research-is-in-a-four-letter-word-that-starts-with-f-is-the-real-secret-to-ultimate-human-performance/#4b1bf28b227f.

99 *MTV News.* "Gymnastics Have Changed for the Better | Rio Olympics | MTV News." August 15, 2016. Video, 0:49. https://www.youtube.com/watch?v=btHeD_uVLLI.

100 Zachos, Elaina. "See What It's Like to Ride the Tallest Wave Ever Surfed." *National Geographic.* April 30, 2018. https://www.nationalgeographic.com/news/2018/04/surf-biggest-wave-record-breaking-award-culture-spd/.

101 Ryan, Tom. *Chosen Suffering: Becoming Elite in Life and Leadership.* Powell, OH: Author Academy Elite, 2020.

102 Two Scoops of Business. "How To Get Into The Flow State." December 2, 2017. https://twoscoopsofbusiness.com/how-to-get-into-the-flow-state.

103 Sleeping At Last. "Sleeping At Last - 'Saturn' (Official Music Video)." June 28, 2016. Video, 4:49. https://www.youtube. com/watch?v=dzNvk80XY9s.

104 Wikipedia. "Autotelic." Accessed July 3, 2020. https:// en.wikipedia.org/wiki/Autotelic.

105 Kennedy, John F. "Address at Rice University on the Nation's Space Effort." Speech, Rice University, Houston, TX, September 12, 1962.

106 Walsh, Michael. "Diana Nyad reveals what was going through her head during 53-hour 'Xtreme dream' swim." *New York Daily News.* September 4, 2013. https://www.nydailynews. com/news/national/diana-nyad-opens-xtreme-dream-swi m-cuba-florida-article-1.1445880.

107 Santos, Jefferson. *Higher Life Design: Arriving at Your Intended Destination Healthy, Wealthy, and Happy.* New York, NY: Morgan James Publishing, 2015.

108 Simon Reece - Topic. "As My Heart Sings." October 25, 2015. Video, 12:04. https://www.youtube.com/ watch?v=EtFdgkzoFM4.

109 Sharma, Raja. *Walt Whitman's Poetry: An Analytical Approach.* 2010.

110 Mangold, James. *Walk the Line.* Burbank, CA: Fox 2000 Pictures, 2005.

111 Wikipedia. "*The Tree of Life* (film)." Accessed July 9, 2020. https://en.wikipedia.org/wiki/The_Tree_of_Life_(film).

112 Lane, Anthony. "Time Trip: Terrence Malick's 'The Tree of Life.'" *The New Yorker.* May 30, 2011. https://www.newyorker. com/magazine/2011/05/30/time-trip.

113 Sandhu, Sukhdev. "The Tree Of Life, review." *The Telegraph.* July 7, 2011. https://www.telegraph.co.uk/culture/film/ filmreviews/8623873/The-Tree-Of-Life-review.html.

114 Marshall, Lee. "The Tree Of Life." *Screen Daily.* May 16, 2011. https://www.screendaily.com/the-tree-of-life/5027636.article.

115 Fischer, Russ. "Early Buzz: Terrence Malick's 'The Tree of Life.'" Slash Film. May 16, 2011. https://www.slashfilm.com/ early-buzz-terrence-malicks-the-tree-life/.

116 Zeitchik, Steven. "David Lynch says he doesn't have any ideas for a new film." *Los Angeles Times.* June 22, 2012. https://www. latimes.com/entertainment/movies/la-xpm-2012-jun-22-l a-et-mn-david-lynch-has-no-ideas-for-a-new-film-20120622- story.html.

117 Freewheeling4. "'Creating the Spectacle!' Online - Part 1 - Finding Freedom." August 17, 2012. Video, 4:43. https://www. youtube.com/watch?v=IPh533ht5AU.

118 Sullivan, Dan. "How to Harness the Power of Negative Thinking." Strategic Coach®. Accessed July 4, 2020. https:// resources.strategiccoach.com/the-multiplier-mindset-blog/ how-to-harness-the-power-of-negative-thinking.

ACKNOWLEDGMENTS

These amazing people create a space conducive for me to stay Unhackable. I am forever grateful.

My Family: Kelly, Keegan, Isabel, and Addison.

My Team: Abigail Young, Amanda Painter, Angela Dee Smith, Brenda Dunagan, Brenda Haire, Chellie Phillips, Corrie Johnson, Crissy Maier, Daphne Smith, Dave Samuel, David Branderhorst, Debra Hayes, Donna Cowan, Emily Myers, Erica Foster, Faye Bryant, Felicity Fox, Jen Cook, Jenifer Harris, Jill Young, Kelly Renee Baker, Kirsten Samuel, Linda Outka, Lisa Moser, Michael Domeny, Nanette O'Neal, Niccie Kliegl, Sara McDermott, Sheila Davis, Sophie Gardiner, Tanisha Williams, Terri Day, Tina Morlock, and Tony Colson.

UNHACKABLE
CLUB

A sincere thank you to the Unhackable Club members
for their incredible support.

Top 10

Dr. Brandt R. Gibson   BeUnhackable.com

Top 100

Kerry Ahrend, PMP   UnhackableLeadership.com
Jacqueline M. Arnold   UnhackableIn30Days.com
Lynn Baber   UnhackableVision.com
Janet L. Black   UnhackableSuccess.com
Dr. Tony Colson   GetUnhackable.com
Cheri Dotterer   UnhackableCourageAcademy.com
Mackenzie Flohr   UnhackableCreator.com
Lisa Frattali   UnhackableDestinies.com
Karen Gibbs   UnhackableHope.com.au
Sarah B. Grandstaff   BuildUnhackableTeams.com
Dr. Jim Henry   UnhackableLifeGivers.life
Michelle Klaseen   UnhackableCourage.life
Niccie Kliegl   UnhackableChristian.com
Jeffrey A. Kramer   PerfectlyUnhackable.com
Sally Livingston, LMFT   UnhackableMe.com
Christine Maier   UnhackableStory.com
Marty Mitchell   LiveUnhackable.com
Chellie W. Phillips   UnhackableEmployee.com
Shari Rickenbach   UnhackableVoiceAndValue.com
Laura Stewart Shortridge   UnhackableDreams.com
Betty Jewell Slater   TheUnhackableLeader.com
Daphne V. Smith   UnhackableHope.com
Doreen Steenland   UnhackableMoms.com
Vicki Terrill, CPLC   TheUnhackables.com
Renee Vidor   UnhackableCoaching.com
Travis M. White   TheUnhackableMind.com

UnhackableBook.com/club

ABOUT THE AUTHOR

Kary Oberbrunner is igniting souls. Through his writing, speaking, and coaching, he helps individuals and organizations clarify who they are, why they're here, and where they should invest their time and energy.

Kary struggled to find his own distinct voice and passion. As a young man, he suffered from severe stuttering, depression, and self-injury. Today a transformed man, Kary equips people to experience Unhackability in work and life and share their message with the world. In the past twenty years, he's ignited over one million people with his content. He lives in Ohio with his wife, Kelly, and three children: Keegan, Isabel, and Addison.

Connect at KaryOberbrunner.com

**the elite full-service branding experience
that increases your credibility & authority**

EthosCollective.vip

About Igniting Souls

We believe:

Clarity attracts. Confusion repels.

There are two types of people in the world:
those that let the world happen to them and those
that happen to the world. Although a subtle difference,
this makes all the difference.

The glory of God is a person fully alive.
We were created to show up filled up.

The most powerful weapon on earth is the human soul on fire.
The most damaging thing in the life of a child is the
unlived life of a parent.

Souls on Fire know WHO they are (identity),
WHY they're here (purpose), and WHERE they're going (direction).

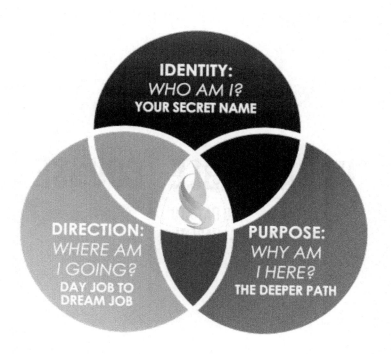

You've read *Unhackable*.
Now it's time to take the online course.

UNHACKABLE COURSE

30 DAYS TO
EXPERIENCING UNHACKABLITY
IN WORK AND LIFE

Learn More
UnhackableBook.com/Course

BECOME A CERTIFIED UNHACKABLE COACH

Get Paid to Help People Close their Gaps
Between Dreaming and Doing

Learn More
UnhackableBook.com/Coach

You don't get what you want—you get who you are.
And who you are is determined by how you think.

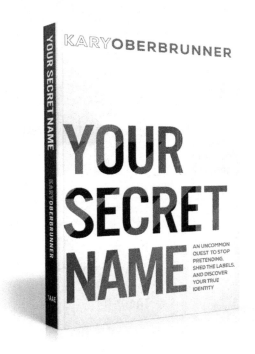

Get Your Free Copy
YourSecretName.com
plus shipping & handling | while supplies last

Don't live another day without knowing your purpose.

Get Your Free Copy
DeeperPathBook.com
plus shipping & handling | while supplies last

Go as you please, earn as you wish, and live as you like.
Start doing your dream job today!

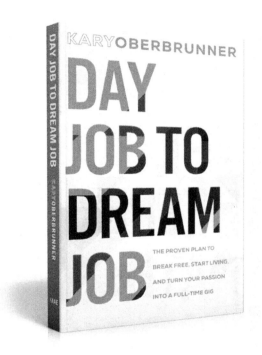

Get Your Free Copy
DayJobToDreamJob.com
plus shipping & handling | while supplies last

Everything can be hacked, even the truth.

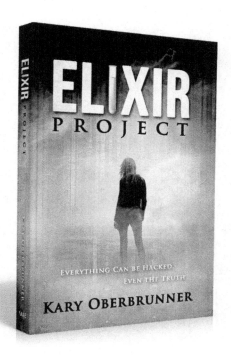

Get Your Free Copy
ElixirProjectBook.com
plus shipping & handling | while supplies last

The Formula to Achieve Bigger Goals
Through Accelerating Teamwork

Learn More
StrategicCoach.com

Made in the USA
Monee, IL
12 June 2021